ARCHITECTURE

Christoph... ...d classical archaeology,
prehistory ... ...te in 1990. He is
... ...orld.

ARCHITECTURE

Christoph Höcker

Front cover from left to right and from top to bottom:

Chrysler Building, New York. Photo: Jochen Tack/Das Fotoarchiv Essen / *The Tower of Babel* Painting by Pieter Brueghel the Elder. Kunsthistorisches Museum, Vienna / Nôtre-Dame-du-Haut in Ronchamp, France, by Le Corbusier. Photo: Dirk Austmann, Cologne / Chambord Castle in the Loire Valley. Photo: Manfred Linke/laif, Cologne / Guggenheim Museum in Bilbao by Frank O. Gehry. Photo: Miguel Gonzalez/laif, Cologne / Palazzo Strozzi in Florence / Floorplan of the Cologne Cathedral / The Sphinx in front of the Pyramid of Cheops in Giza. Photo: Hans Günter Semsek, Cologne / Walter Gropius in front of his entry for the Chicago Tribune Building competition, 1922 / Taj Mahal. Photo: Hans-Joachim Aubert, Bonn / Étienne-Louis Boullée, design for the cenotaph in honor of the physicist Sir Isaac Newton, exterior. Sketch from 1784.

Back cover from top to bottom:

Workers on top of the Empire State Building. Photo: AKG, Berlin / Temple of Castor and Pollux in Rome, detail. From: Henry Parke, *A Drawing of a Student Measuring the Temple of Castor and Pollux in Rome, Made to Illustrate the Corinthian Order for Soane's Royal Academy Lectures*, 1819. The Trustees of Sir John Soane's Museum / The Church of Maria Laach.

Frontispiece: The Glass Pyramid in front of the Louvre, Paris. Photo: W. Spitta, Loham

First published in Great Britain in 2000 by Laurence King Publishing
an imprint of Calmann & King Ltd
71 Great Russell Street
London
WC1B 3BP
Tel: +44 20 7831 6351
Fax: +44 20 7831 8356
e-mail: enquiries@calmann-king.co.uk
www.laurence-king.com

Text copyright © 2000 DuMont Buchverlag GmbH und Co. Kommanditgesellschaft, Köln, Germany
Copyright © 2000 English language translation, Barron's Educational Series, Inc.
English text version by: Editorial Office Martin Sulzer-Reichel, Overath, Germany
Translated by: Sally Schreiber, Köln, Germany
Edited by: Tammi Reichel, Overath, Germany

A catalogue record for this book is available from the British Library

ISBN 1 85669 159 4

Printed in Italy by Editoriale Lloyd

Contents

Preface

What is architecture, really? And what can a Concise History explain about it? These may seem like trivial questions, but it is useful to consider them briefly at the outset of this work, especially since the tendency of many recent books on architecture has been to present selections, at best, offering a summary of historical and present-day forms, and have often remained caught in a Western perspective.

Since prehistoric times, architecture has fulfilled basic human needs, for example, the building of houses. But at the same time, the possibility to create designs of excessive size or elaborate magnificence has allowed architecture to put itself at the service of individuals, groups, or entire communities as a medium of self-aggrandizement and display. Furthermore, unlike the crafting of a stone axe or a clay pot, architecture is almost always a collective rather than an individual effort—a goal-oriented, creative activity of a group of people operating within a specific historical environment. For this reason, architecture through the ages is by no means merely a category of formal art history, but has always formed an important aspect of the social history of the human race, as well.

The present volume attempts to do justice to the understanding of architecture in this larger sense. In addition to a tour of architectural "highlights" throughout history, this book also presents the story of corrugated hut settlements and pre-fab panel constructions, poor wattle-and-daub cottages, and the fortresses of robber barons clinging to rocky crevices—in other words, not just "noble" architecture, but also its more everyday aspects. The working conditions of the architects is a theme, as are various building technologies, the development of new building materials, and finally, the requirements of people in their given architectural surroundings. Naturally, in addition to the historical perspective, this book also takes a good look at the present—including issues such as the position of postmodernism within the history of architecture, designs for a radical utopia, and the inhumanity of the concept of a "machine for living."

Christoph Höcker, Augsburg, April 2000

Ziggurat, city, royal fortress

Any attempt to discuss the architecture of the advanced
civilizations of the Middle East is an immense task. A
summary of all architectural phenomena in the area
encompassing Mesopotamia (present-day Iraq), Iran,
Asia Minor, and Syria between ca. 3300 and 800 BC is
equivalent to a review of the civilized world during this
period. This "cradle of civilization" gave rise to numerous architectural developments that pointed the way to
the future—developments achieved by subsequent cultures only much later, if at all. By the 6th millennium
BC, that is, in pre-historic times, farming and herding
had progressed to an extent that allowed the permanent
Anatolian settlement of Çatal Hüyük, the world's first
urban "metropolis." With urban development came the
first large-scale functional architecture, at a time when
Stone Age hunters and gatherers were still the dominant cultures in Europe and the Americas.

The rural Sumerian culture of Mesopotamia, in the
so-called fertile crescent between the Euphrates and
Tigris Rivers in present-day Iraq, gave rise to competitive metropolitan-like centers beginning as early as
4000 BC. The city of Uruk took form in the 4th–3rd
millennium BC, followed by Ur in the 3rd–2nd millennium BC. The clay brick ruins of Uruk, discovered
by a European expedition in 1849, underwent wide-
scale excavation by the German Orient Society beginning in 1912. The remains show that Uruk was the
capital city of a highly developed economy, with specialized labor and a centrally organized monarchical
government. A six-mile-long city wall protects the
numerous small domestic buildings and warehouses
that surround the impressive center of the city. The city
shows evidence of quick growth. Around 3300 BC, the
settlement of 40,000 inhabitants covered almost 500
acres; 500 years later, the population had reached more
than 70,000, and the city, which now stretched over an
area of more than 1,350 acres, had been repeatedly
enclosed in new and larger defensive walls. Numerous
clay tablets with cuneiform writing prove a high level

of administrative technology, including the ability to archive quantities of information.

The city served as a depot for grain, weapons, and all varieties of trade goods, and at the center of the settlement stood the ziggurat (1), a high irregular structure, at times in the form of a stepped pyramid, at

other times tower-like or shaped like a podium whose uppermost platform served as a site for the temple. The precise function of these ziggurats that rise so strikingly from a flat landscape is unclear, although they are found in every large city throughout Mesopotamia. City centers also contained large and impressive palaces. As early as the 3rd millennium BC, the artfully constructed clay brick architecture created perfectly formed arches by using a supporting scaffold during building and removing it afterward (2). The principle behind such arches remained unknown in the West until the 4th century BC, when it was rediscovered and put to use by Hellenic-Greek architecture.

[1] An artificially created height rising in the midst of a flat landscape: the ziggurat of Uruk (Iraq), 4th millennium BC.

The ruins of Ur, located south of Uruk, also lay in the shadow of an immense ziggurat (3). Here, too, were

[2] Brick architecture with half-round arches. Palace of Uruk, 3rd millennium BC.

remains of a large palace complex and many domestic and utility buildings, in addition to a large necropolis containing shaft graves and architecturally designed mausoleums in the shape of houses with an underground vault.

From the 2nd millennium BC, the Indo-European Hittites increasingly made their way into the Middle East as aggressive conquerors. The core of the Hittite Empire was initially Anatolia, with its large fortified capital, Hattushash,

[3] The great ziggurat of Ur (Iraq) dating from the late 4th millennium BC, as seen during the excavations conducted in 1922 by the British archeologist Leonard Wolley.

located approximately 90 miles east of present-day Ankara. The site was discovered in 1834 by Charles Texier near the village Bogazkale, and was completely excavated in the course of several campaigns beginning in 1907. The Hittite state was a monarchy with feudal characteristics. Its king also served as the high cult priest, and the nobility as well as the officials took part in all political, military, and religious decisions. This political-social structure was manifest in the architectural appearance of the capital, which was divided into an upper and lower city (4). In the center stood the king's palace, with its fortress-like defenses. To the

[4] Layout of the Hittite capital of Hattushash. Excavation as of 1988.

north and south, temple complexes towered over houses, workshops, and storage buildings, as well as commercial quarters for the many foreign traders who had taken up residence there.

Raised earthen structures are, in fact, a typical architectural and settlement form found in various Middle Eastern cultures, especially along the Levant coast: the *tell* (Arabic for hillock) was an immense mound (artificially created in flat regions) that offered enough room for the entire settlement and could be well secured against attack with palisades and ditches.

Pyramids and temples: Architecture in ancient Egypt

Today's image of ancient Egyptian culture rests primarily on the monumental and largely well-preserved architecture of the ancient civilization. Egyptian temples, tombs, and pyramids—often containing "secret" hieroglyphic writing—are the much admired structures of a society whose unusual customs and rites have lent it an aura of mystery. This admiring stance often overlooks the fact that the gigantic remains of ancient Egyptian architecture in fact represent only a small portion of the buildings that once existed. Most Egyptian buildings, especially the domestic structures and workshops devoted to every-day purposes, were inevitably constructed of much less durable materials than the stone used for the great monuments. More mundane architecture was built of unbaked bricks formed from the silt of the Nile and from reeds or other herbaceous material. The only buildings that have survived, however, were those of virtually indestructible material, such as stone blocks. As a result, the image of ancient Egyptian architecture as a mirror of the entire Egyptian culture is deceptive. Just how common and widespread the architecture of herbaceous materials was can be clearly seen from the ornamentation of stone buildings that have endured: One often finds motifs, on columns, for example, deriving from natural materials that have been carried over from the original material into stone architectural forms (5). Unfortunately, little remains of the numerous, rigidly geometrical domestic complexes that consisted of buildings up to three stories high, or of the broadly laid-out palaces with their gardens and ponds.

Under the ancient Egyptian pharaohs, monumental structures made of permanent building materials existed as early as 2600 BC in two forms, both deeply implicated in reflecting the Egyptian state: tombs and temples. The leading form of Egyptian tomb is the pyramid, a grandiose and dignified structure originally reserved for the kings, and even later primarily limited to royalty. The pyramid form only gradually developed into a geometrical ideal; in the beginning there were terraced monuments such as the step pyramids of Djoser near Sakkara, built around 2650 BC. The ideal

[5] Columns as an imitation of nature: various columns with palm, lotus, or papyrus motifs from ancient Egyptian tombs and temples. Reconstructions.

Ancient Architecture of the

Pyramids and Temples:

[6] The pyramid field of Giza, ca. 2500 BC: The pyramids of Cheops and Chephren with their subsidiary structures. Reconstructed drawing from the 19th century.

form of the pyramid based on a square ground plan had already been developed in the 3rd millennium BC, and by the end of the Old Kingdom (ca. 2100 BC) more than 20 major specimens had been built. The famed pyramid fields of Giza near Cairo (6) contain the two largest pyramids ever built, those of Cheops and Chephren. The pyramid of Cheops (reigned ca. 2545–2520 BC) rises from a base of almost 750 feet on each side to a height of nearly 780 feet; the pyramid of Chephren (7; reigned ca. 2510–1485 BC), with a height and a side length of almost 470 feet, is hardly less imposing. With a total volume of more than 3.5 million cubic yards, the Cheops pyramid is still among the largest structures ever erected in human history.

Approximately ten smaller pyramids have been identified dating from the period of the Middle Kingdom (ca. 2100–1551 BC). In contrast to those of the Old Kingdom, however, they are built not of solid stone, but of clay bricks supported by a skeleton of stone. The pyramids of the New Kingdom (1551–1080 BC) are considerably smaller and were also used as tombs for officials. The large pyramids of the Old Kingdom were not

[7] Although many of the facing panels of the pyramid of Chephren (near Giza) have fallen away, the upper level of the pyramid still retains its original facade. The panels served to give the originally stepped pyramid a smooth surface.

isolated, but stood with other structures including at least a mortuary temple, a reception area, and an imposing entry ramp—all of which played a part in burial rituals. Often there were also lesser pyramids that might serve as a tomb for the queen, for example. Within the pyramid itself was usually a well-secured burial chamber.

The considerable size of the pyramids meant that construction extended over many years, and typically a pharaoh ordered the work on "his" pyramid to begin immediately after taking the throne. The construction was directed by experts and specialized workers who had command of technology, including ramps and scaffolds. The labor itself was carried out not by slaves, but by free field workers who owed work service during the dry and flood seasons. The construction of the pyramids carried with it a social and political dimension. On the one hand, it provided paid work for peasants during the seasons when field work was impossible, thus serving the good of the workers; on the other

hand, it served also the kingdom, which thus remained safe from political unrest.

[8] The walled temple of Karnak by Thebes. The areas of the gods Mont, Amun, and Mut. Reconstruction works.

In contrast to the pyramids, the high point of Egyptian temple construction was reached in the Middle and New Kingdoms, with most of the complexes stemming from the 2nd millennium BC. Historically, temples developed from simple wattle structures into buildings of monumental size. Immense walled temple complexes such as that of Karnak near Thebes (8) contributed to the architectural profile of the Nile valley during the 18th dynasty (early New Kingdom, after 1551 BC). The temple itself was laid out as a rectangle, usually symmetrical around an axis, and was divided into numerous chambers and passages. An imposing

[9] The columned hall of the temple at Luxor, built in the time of Ramses II. (19th dynasty, 1279–1212 BC).

columned front marked the entrance on the narrow side of the temple (9). This design—familiar from the Horus temple of Edfu, a new Hellenistic construction dating from ca. 200 BC that was based on a considerably older construction—could be expanded almost indefinitely by means of additions. At Heliopolis, for example, the site of the largest such complex in ancient Egypt, the temple covered an area of more than 10.7 million square feet.

Between Orient and Occident: Minoan and Mycenaean palaces of the Bronze Age

The Minoan culture, whose name derives from the legendary King Minos of Crete, extended across the southern Aegean islands in the 2nd millennium BC, with important centers on the islands of Crete and Thera (Santorini). In spite of the geographical proximity to the southern Balkan peninsula, neither Minoan art and culture, nor society nnor religion, were oriented in that direction. The Minoans looked rather to the cultures of the advanced civilizations to the south and southeast, and developed intensive trade relations and cultural contacts with Egypt, the Near East and Asia Minor, and Cyprus.

Whether the basis of power for the Minoan cultures —as described by the Greek historian Thucydides in the 5th century BC—consisted of maritime supremacy (thalassocracy) in the south Aegean is now under question. In any case, it is certain that there must have been a number of highly effective political and military factors that enabled the Minoan people to erect prosperous cities, settlements and palaces without protective walls.

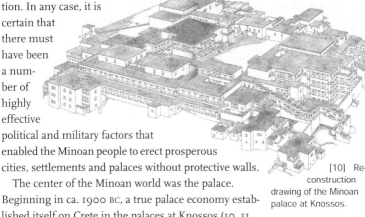

[10] Reconstruction drawing of the Minoan palace at Knossos.

The center of the Minoan world was the palace. Beginning in ca. 1900 BC, a true palace economy established itself on Crete in the palaces at Knossos (10, 11, 12), Kato Zagros, Phaistos, and Mallia. Constructed around a central courtyard, the palace was a multifunctional architectural conglomerate. Several stories high, the labyrinthine interlocking rooms offered storage areas, workshops, living quarters and impressive formal chambers, as well as areas for religious observances and cult rituals. The economic, religious, and social streams of life flowed together in the palace, in traditional oriental fashion, as found in the large palace cities of Babylon. As a result, a system of writing also arose. The sequentially developed Cretan Linear A and Linear B scripts were, like the cuneiform writing of the Sumerians, archival scripts developed in the context of administering a palace economy. In the area surrounding the palaces, as well as somewhat further afield, various urban settlements and generously laid out formal villas indicate enormous material prosperity, unsurpassed craftsmanship, and technical abilities beyond that evident in the surviving remains of architecture and construction. This high level of development is reflected in

[11] Floor plan of the Minoan palace at Knossos showing the spatial organization of the various functions.

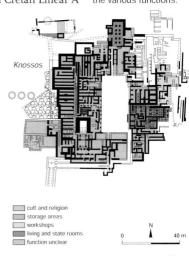

Knossos

cult and religion
storage areas
workshops
living and state rooms
function unclear

N

0   40 m

the frescos, sculpture, jewels, faience work, ceramics, metal implements, and golden jewelry of Minoan civilization.

This charming and peaceful impression of the Minoan culture, which has repeatedly fascinated and inspired the world, stood in stark contrast to the largely contemporaneous Mycenaean culture on the Greek main-land. As an offshoot of mid-European Bronze Age cul-tures, the hallmark of the Mycenaean culture was ad-vanced weapons technology. Along with their practical but rather artless ceramics, war implements forged of hard bronze alloys—daggers, long and short swords, armor, and helmets—are the main threads of the Mycenaean cul-ture as found in numerous graves dating between 1800 and 1100 BC. The Mycenaean fortress-palace was organized similarly to that of the Mino-ans, and can best be seen today in Argolis (Mycenae,

[12]   The palace of Knossos on Crete has been partially recon-structed (work begun by English archaeologist Sir Arthur Evans in 1900), giving the modern viewer an interesting perspec-tive that blends ruins and buildings.

Tiryns), the Peloponese (Pylos), Attica (Athens), and Boeotia (Orchomenos, Thebes, Gla). The palaces were not only the seat of the ruler, but also epicenters for all kinds of social and economic activity. They functioned as centers of production, provided storage sites for raw materials, and offered loci for trade as well as for political and religious ceremonies.

And yet, there were important differences. Unlike the Cretan palaces that remained peaceful through the centuries, the Mycenaean centers more typically dis-play a strong sense of competition. Surrounded by solid defensive walls made of fitted polygonal stone blocks (Cyclopean walls), Mycenaean palaces were in fact highly fortified bastions (13), arising not only in response to unfriendly threats from the outside, but particulary in answer to on-going feuds among the various palaces. The Minoan cultures of the southern Aegean were fundamentally oriented toward general cooperation and commonality; within the Mycenaean fortresses, diplomacy and coalitions were hardly foreign terms, but on the whole, a state of war prevailed. Every clan sought first

[13] Excavated ruins of the Mycenaean fortress of Tiryns in Argolis, a strongly fortified Mycenaean princely seat erected on a raised area, ideally suited for control of the surrounding farmland. Aerial view.

and foremost its own benefit. One might well imagine the social system of a fortress-city such as Mycenae in terms of a privileged clan of perhaps 100 members ruling from inside the fortress and a dependent population living in scattered villages throughout the surrounding area. Always situated on a hill, the fortress could easily control an area extending from one to six miles; at the same time, the fortress offered the population safety in case of attack.

The reasons for the decline of the Mycenaean and Minoan cultures at the end of the 2nd millennium BC is still not known in detail. The Minoans on Crete were presumably conquered by the mainland Mycenaeans, who were in turn suppressed by new immigrants.

[14] Shaft graves in the fortress-palace of Mycenae. Mid-2nd millennium BC

17

Architecture and building technology in ancient Greece

It is almost impossible to overestimate the influence of Greco-Roman architecture down through the ages. Its impact is evident not only in the many adaptations of ancient classical models throughout subsequent history (see page 84ff., 114ff.), but also in language itself: The word "architecture" derives from the Latin word *architectura*, which originally denoted the planning and design related to the construction of buildings. Vitruvius's *De architectura libri decem* (*Ten Books of Architecture*), written during the reign of Augustus at the turn of the millennium, formulate a comprehensive historical view of the roots of architecture and is still read today.

Numerous well-preserved inscriptions from the late 5th and 4th centuries BC provide invaluable insights into the building and design processes in ancient Greece and Rome. These inscriptions, which originally served for records and accounts, indicate that construction in ancient Greece was a highly complex process, rooted deeply in the social fabric. For example, information gleaned from these inscriptions documents that even the construction of a relatively small structure, such as the temple of Aesculapius at Epidaurus in the 4th century BC, constituted a great challenge to both planners and artisans. The shape and design of a building were determined only after long and sometimes heated debate by those who commissioned the temple—that is, by the priests or the city itself. In this initial process, the architect played no role as an autonomous artist, but merely drew up a "blue print" to serve as a construction guide in conformity with the decisions of the commissioners. Only then did the architect, together with a committee of city officials or priests responsible for deadlines and costs, assume responsibility for the concrete organizational planning. The entire project was subdivided into numerous construction phases, ranging from very small to comprehensive. As in modern practice, "contracts" were distributed to individual artisans or workshops for completion of a certain phase. Whereas in the 6th and 5th centuries BC numerous small workshops were generally involved in the building of a temple, the 4th century saw a rise in large firms that often subcontracted portions of their work to other firms. After about 300 BC, in very large projects whose date of completion could not easily be calculated, permanent quarters were erected to house the workers and equipment, as in the construction of the Hellenistic temple to Apollo at Didyma, near Miletus in Asia Minor.

The recipients of construction contracts were wholly responsible for the execution of the building stages they had taken over, with particular emphasis laid on meeting the predetermined deadlines. Each contractor had to provide a guarantor—someone to stand surety—in case of delay or default, for relatively steep penalties were imposed for tardiness. Apparently, this was a common problem, because a considerable portion of the estimated building costs was usually allotted to prospective fines for delayed work. Furthermore, because the contract costs were fixed from the outset, the contractor assumed sole responsibility for any possible cost overruns. The inscriptions further indicate that the cost of procuring building materials was substantially more than that for manual labor at the construction site. In the case of the temple to Aesculapius at Epidaurus, the material had to be brought from a great distance and was transported in part by ship. Even when teams of five to seven stone masons worked on the fluting of a single column for up to two months, as in the Erechtheum on the Acropolis in Athens, manual labor remained a negligible factor in the total expense of the building. Daily wages were exceedingly low, just a *drachma* per day for free or slave labor. (In the latter case, the money of course went to the slave owner.)

336–323 BC
Reign of Alexander the Great; conquest of Persia; Alexander's empire dissolves into the Diadochi kingdoms after his death

264–241 BC
First of three Punic Wars between Rome and Carthage; Rome conquers Sicily

from 171 BC
Rome conquers Greece

146 BC
Destruction of Corinth and Carthage

from 49 BC
Civil war in Italy; 44 BC: assassination of Caesar

from 27 BC
Reign of Augustus (Principate)

AD 14
Death of Augustus; Tiberius succeeds to the Principate; beginning of imperial Roman age

3rd century AD
Crisis in the Roman empire (dispute over succession, secession, economic decline)

after AD 284
Restoration of Roman empire under the tetrarchy established by Diocletian

[15] Transport of a stone block weighing several tons by means of reusable wooden wheels—an invention ascribed to architects Chersiphron and Metagenes, active in the construction of the Artemiseum of Ephesus in the 6th century BC. Reconstruction.

19

[16] Paradigm for the Corinthian capital of the round temple (*tholos*) at the shrine of Aesculapius at Epidauros, built between 360 and 310 BC. The paradigm, which served as a precise model for the serial carving of all the marble capitals, was buried next to the building upon completion as an offering. Epidauros Museum.

The transportation of material and the positioning of building segments required special equipment such as rollers, casters, carts, crowbars, and mobile cranes (15). Usually the individual stone units were roughly shaped into their final form at the quarry. Stone blocks, as well as the drums, or sections, of columns, were hewn close to their required size, but left a little larger than the final dimensions in order to provide a "protective layer" around the pieces. That was struck away later on the building site in case damage occurred during transport. At the construction site itself, the precise form of the structural unit was chiseled according to a set model (*paradeigma*). Capitals (16), for example, were fashioned serially and then set into position by means of block and tackle or levers (17). Especially in the case of brittle marble or limestone, in order to minimize damage to the individual stone units at this stage of construction, anathyrosis was used to minimize contact between the surfaces of different pieces. The large stone blocks of the walls and stepped base (*crepidoma*) as well as beams were held fast by bronze staples, and stone drum units were secured with dowels. Only after the elements were set into their final positions was the outer layer of marble removed; the columns then received their fluting, and the entire structure was given a coating of bright, colorful paint.

From today's standpoint, ancient Greek architecture seems to have consisted mainly of limestone and marble columns and blocks—that is, of temples, halls, etc. But this conclusion is in fact a cliché resulting from the survival of precisely these buildings into the

[17] Illustration of various techniques to raise building components. Initially hoisting bosses, i.e., stone projections around which rope could be wound, were left in place. When the work was done they were usually chiseled away. On unfinished buildings they are sometimes still visible today. The stone blocks were shaped on site with extreme precision.

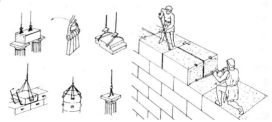

present in relatively good condition. The majority of ancient Greek buildings, however, were constructed of fragile, non-durable materials such as wood and clay. At best, all that remains of these structures are the ruins of solid foundations and bases; only in rare cases have portions of walls survived. As can be seen in the ruins of the city wall of Athens (18), however, building techniques involving clay were common not only for insignificant huts and stables, but also for stately architectural works meant to display the grandeur of the city, and even for fortifications.

[18] A wall made of clay bricks set upon a stable sockel of stone blocks: The Athenian city wall at Kerameikos, ca. 1900.

Types of ancient classical architecture—a survey

In contrast to modern architecture, which has an almost unlimited repertoire of architectonic forms at its disposal, architecture of the ancient world was essentially limited to a few specific types. This concentration on a small number of forms is even more true of classical Roman than of ancient Greek architecture. The spectrum of ancient temple design was thus formally circumscribed. In addition to the standard peristyle (colonnaded) temple, which might be varied in a number of ways (see page 24ff.), circular temples were also a part of the Greek repertoire, as seen at Delphi or Epidauros, for example. Temple design also encompassed an array of smaller, less stately antae temples (that is, with strengthened columns at the ends of the walls, but without a peristyle). The altars incorporated into these temples were not always discrete architectural structures, but might consist of anything from a mound of ashes at the offering site, to roughly hewn stone benches or simple table-and-bench combinations, all the way to monumental structures, such as the large altar to Zeus at Pergamon. Roman temples are characterized by a solid base with a wide exterior

[19] Plan of the temple at Orvieto, 5th century BC. Such Etruscan buildings served as the model for Roman podium temples, which clearly distinguished themselves in form and structure from the Greek peristyle temples.

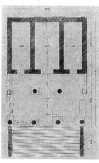

[20] The Attalos Stoa in Athens, built in 140 BC, was a gift of King Attalos II of Pergamon to the city. Reconstructed during the 1950s with exact attention to details, it is an example of a Greek colonnaded hall that was used as a marketplace.

[21] The Roman theater built in the 2nd century AD in Aspendos, Turkey, is the best surviving example of this ancient architectural type.

flight of stairs leading to the front of the temple (19). In contrast to the Greek structures, the Roman temple was oriented in a single direction. In the capitol temples of the cities the *cella*, or chamber, in the interior was usually divided into three parts in honor of the capitol trinity: Here the gods Jupiter, Juno, and Minerva were revered.

Greek column and stone-block architecture as manifested in the peristyle temples was slowly expanded to apply to other buildings as well. Among these were the stately fountain structures that begin to appear in the 5th century BC, richly decorated entry gates (for example, the Propylaea of the Acropolis in Athens), and long covered halls (20). With the advent of Hellenistic architecture in the 3rd to 1st centuries BC, a fundamental change took place. Now, multistory architectural structures with complex, fenestrated wall surfaces were constructed on a variety of ground plans with an eye to practical utility.

In the Greco-Roman world, recreational architecture—that is, structures devoted to entertainment—played an important part in the society. In Greece, theaters were not only places for dramatic performances but also served as the loci of political forums or as conference sites for the populace. Embedded into the steep surrounding hillsides, Greek theaters typically made use of the natural terrain; Roman theaters, in contrast, were erected as freestanding constructions (21). But both theater forms shared a similar internal

structure consisting of an ascending *cavea* (seating rows for spectators) and an *orchestra* (place of action), that is, a formal stage with a multistoried building at the back. One variation of the Roman theater was the *odeon*, a small, completely roofed theater intended for poetry readings and music performances (for example, the Odeon of Herodes Atticus on the southern slope of the Athenian Acropolis).

The Roman amphitheater and circus are also directly indebted to the Roman theater and acting culture. The Colosseum in Rome (22), whose gigantic oval form epitomizes the amphitheaters which were later to spring up in almost every large city under the Roman emperors, was based on the wooden tribunal structures customarily built in Roman cities for gladiatorial games into the 1st century BC. Because citizens of higher rank wished to avoid the excesses of the crowds who thronged to these enormously popular festivities, the privileged class found ways of blocking the construction of more permanent stone amphitheater structures from the cities for centuries. When, however, the building of such a structure became inevitable, the amphitheater was usually relegated to the outskirts of the city for reasons of security. The Roman circus, whose archetypal form is seen in the Circus Maximus in Rome, can be traced back to the Greek Hippodrome, which hosted wagon races and served as both the start and finish of large processions and parades.

Another form of ancient classical recreational architecture was the thermal bath—the public baths, or *thermae*, which also offered additional sports and entertainment facilities. Initially, the baths were rather modest, as seen for example in Pompeii; but during the height of the empire (ca. 100 BC to AD 100), they developed into stately regal structures, constituting a magnificent "gift" to the people. The large Roman *thermae*, built by the emperors Titus, Caracalla, and Diocletian, among others, were constructed on a palatial scale and were characterized by magnificent imperial opulence (see page 31). Often integrated into

[22] The Roman Colosseum: the archetypal amphitheater. Engraving from the 18th century.

the baths were various older architectural structures, such as those ancient Greek forms of sport architecture, the gymnasium (for general physical training) and the *palestra* (for wrestling).

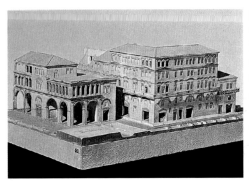

[23] Four-story rental house in the harbor city of Ostia, dating from the 2nd century AD. Model reconstruction.

The basic design of the ancient Greek or Roman house (see page 27) was eventually expanded by a number of forms drawn from urban as well as country traditions. In the densely populated inner cities, high-rise rental houses of up to six stories were built (23). Another Roman "invention" was the villa—in its original form, the buildings of a country farm. During the 1st century BC, however, the villa increasingly took on the trappings of the entertainment and recreational architecture preferred by the Roman upper class (see page 31).

The Greek peristyle temple

To modern eyes, no building more typically embodies classical Greek architecture than the colonnaded temple whose core (*cella*) and surrounding columned walkway are mounted on a long, stepped podium or

[24] Building structure of a Doric temple
1 stepped base (sockel)
2 stylobate **3** columns of the peristasis
4 architrave **5** metope-triglyph frieze
6 tympanon
7 acroterion **8** antefixa
9 roof timbers **10** columns in the entry hall
11 pronaos (entry hall to the cella) **12** exterior wall of the cella
13 triple-aisle cella
14 adytum (innermost sanctuary)

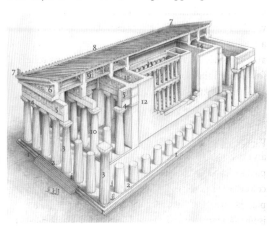

base (*crepidoma*). The Parthenon on the Athenian Acropolis (25), constructed in record time between 449 and 438 BC, is perhaps the most typical example of this type of structure. Buildings like the Parthenon often had nothing to do with the actual worship of a deity, which did not, in fact, constitute an indispensable requisite of a shrine. Temples were used to preserve the images of deities; even when the buildings played an integral role in cult ceremonies, the structure represented a votive gift to the gods rather than a church or synagogue. Such temples were consecrated to the community in a general sense because of their size and cost. Symbolizing the shared understanding and convictions of the community, temples became the focal points of activities ideally suited to strengthen the integration and collective identity of the citizens, especially during the social upheavals in the Greek city-states during the 7th and 6th centuries BC. It is interesting to note how individual inscriptions on column units or drums, roof tiles, or other structural elements were integrated into a larger whole. Hence, the Parthenon functioned not merely as a religious site, but as a votive gift in the larger sense—an extraordinary monument whose numerous reliefs formulated the political and military ambitions of the city-state of Athens.

[25] The west front of the Parthenon on the Athenian Acropolis. The temple with its rows of 8 x 17 columns was built entirely of marble and designed on an unusually large scale. Optically, it is both exceptionally precise and harmonious in its proportions.

No conclusive prototype or rationale has yet been found to explain the form of the peristyle temple, in particular the positioning of the surrounding columns and the orders of decoration. Even though these temples seem so quintessentially Greek today, the earliest colonnaded halls, used in wooden structures (for example, the "temple" of Lefkandi, 10th century BC), are isolated examples. In the late 7th century BC the Doric

[26] The Ionic temple of Artemis at Ephesus. Drawing of a reconstruction of the new temple (essentially based on the archaic building dating from the 6th century BC, which was destroyed by the fire laid by Herostratus in 356 BC). The temple was conceived as a dipteral structure with a double row of columns, suggesting an entire pillared forest to the observer. The lower ends of the shafts were elaborately decorated with sculpted reliefs.

order emerged as a completely developed stone structure (24), occurring primarily on the Greek mainland (Olympia), the western islands (Corfu), and soon in the colonized cities of Sicily and southern Italy. Nevertheless, the Doric order suggests fully developed wooden predecessors that had been translated into stone. Building elements necessary to wooden constructions but technically extraneous to stone—such as nails, rafters and beams, as well as the abacus and fluting of the columns—were incorporated into the stone structures as formal details of high ornamental value.

The Ionic order, whose characteristic shallow-fluted columns were mounted between a protruding base and a volute capital, dispensed with the triglyphs and guttae: Its entablature no longer contained features reminiscent of wooden constructions. The characteristic form of this order was established in approximately the middle of the 6th century BC in the huge archaic temples at Ephesus (26), Didyma, and Samos. The elegant and ornamental Ionic form (and the Corinthian form derived from it beginning in the 4th century BC) completely replaced the older, rougher Doric form after 300 BC. Eventually, new building forms, including circular structures, were added to the architectural repertoire.

In the two centuries between 600 and 400 BC, the Greek peristyle temple underwent significant changes in form. A modular system of building became increasingly common—a natural enough development considering that a Doric peristyle temple, for example, consisted of a limited number of sections and sectional relationships. The distance between columns became more and more regular, and the proportions of individual units as well as the entire structure became more harmonious. With meticulous care, such structural problems as the "Doric angle contraction" (27) were worked out until, at last, the experimental phase ended in ideal models which could be used again and again. For a modern archaeologist, therefore, only a few remains allow an entire Greek temple to be reconstructed. In addition, based on its place in this developmental process, the building can be precisely dated within a few decades.

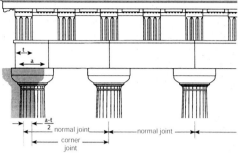

The Greco-Roman house

The desire to demonstrate personal wealth by means of the architectural opulence of their private homes was foreign to the ancient Greeks. The urban population usually carried on its economic and domestic life in relatively simple buildings oriented around central courtyardsffl; extended families or clans typically lived under a single roof that housed their servants and provided room for domestic labor and workshops. The Pastas House (28) represents a common type of dwelling: From the *oikos*, the courtyard, access could be gained to a perpendicularly running corridor (*pastas*) which led to the typically two-storied living quarters. Shops or storage rooms and workshops were positioned around the courtyard.

Architectural luxury first became a noticeable phenomenon in the 4th century BC, when citizens throughout Greece began withdrawing from active participation in the *polis* (city) and retreated into the private sphere. Large peristyle houses arose in which the *andron*, a small room originally designated for the *symposium* (a convivial gathering of men), expanded into a kind of "public" area that was much frequented by visitors and therefore strictly separated from the private rooms. Through the expenditure lavished on the building and on decorative mosaics and frescoes, the andron and peristyle came to indicate the social and economic status of the house owner. In Greek cities, such houses arose one after the other, on

[27] In classical Rome and Greece, the problem of the "Doric angle contraction" constituted one of the major building problems in the ancient world: It was impossible to wrap a symmetrical and proportionate series of triglyphs (t) and metopes (a) around a corner. According to Vitruvius the Ionic order was developed since the conflict could not be solved.

[28] Floor plan of the Pastas House, built ca. 350 BC in the northern Greek city of Olynth.

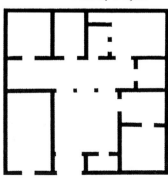

elongated *insula*, or city blocks, that were defined by a grid of streets intersecting at right angles. Initially, all the plots may have been of equal size, but this urban structure was easily modified through the purchase of a neighboring plot and the consequent enlargement of the original house (29).

In Italy, the 4th century BC saw the rise of the type of domestic architecture known as the atrium house (30). Shielded from the street by its outer walls, this one-story dwelling (or occasionally two-story, as in Hercu-laneum) contained a central hall-like area that was roofed over except for a small opening to let in light; the various living quarters were arranged around this atrium. At the back of the house there was usually a small garden plot surrounded by a high wall. The impression that the house was hermetically sealed from the outside world was strengthened by the view from the street, from which usually only a narrow, insignificant entrance led into the house itself. The entry was flanked on both sides by shops which opened to the street but offered no passageway to the house.

Depending on the financial capacities of the owner, this basic domestic architectural concept could be expanded to the dimensions of a city palace, as can be seen in the houses of Pompeii, well preserved by the volcanic eruption of Mt. Vesuvius in the year AD 79. When enough land was available within an *insula*, elements of the atrium house might be combined with those of the Greek-Hellenistic peristyle house. The Casa del Fauno in Pompeii (31), a labyrinthine house of more than 21,500 square feet, contains two atriums and two extensive

[29] In basic design, the row houses in northern Greek Olynthos are all alike. They are built on standardized lots in a square designated as an "island"—an area defined by a grid of perpendicularly laid out streets. Reconstructed model.

[30] Two basic types of Roman houses: The peristyle house, bottom left, comes from the Hellenistic-Greek tradition while the atrium house, bottom right, has Etruscan-Italian roots. In Pompeii a mixture of both types is prevalent.

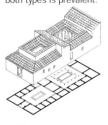

peristyles, one covered with a roof, the second conceived as a garden adjacent to the living areas.

Such houses were usually open to the south, and the rooms were so arranged as to avoid overheating in the summer and to store solar energy in the winter. (Elaborate heating systems were customary only in areas outside the Mediterranean region.) In addition to the structure and size of the house itself, the furnishings also reflected the wealth of the owner. The remains of Pompeii offer a spectrum ranging from very simple wooden furnishings and modest ornamental wall decorations to highly elaborate interiors with candelabra, reclining couches of bronze (*klinen*), filigree work, extensive wall paintings and floor mosaics, statues adorning the peristyle, and ivory or metal furniture ornaments. Costly pillows and materials, embroidery, silver objects, and dishes did not survive but were surely present.

[31] The Casa del Fauno in Pompeii. View into the peristyle garden. The famous mosaic depicting the battle between Alexander the Great and the Persian King Darius was discovered here, in what is sometimes known as the Casa Goethe, in 1832. (Today in the National Museum of Naples.)

Architecture: The mirror of society—innovations in ancient Roman architecture and building techniques

Of all the achievements of ancient Rome, the feats of engineering have proven most fascinating in both the Middle Ages and modern times. Not only the magnificence and size of Roman architecture, but also its durability, technical finesse, and astonishing functionality have elicited continuous admiration. Bridges and roadways, aqueducts, multistoried apartment buildings, immense domed halls, and wide basilicas with barrel vaulting were among the Roman architectural achievements that have functioned as models and inspiration in succeeding centuries. Nor was the influence of these architectural innovations limited to formal inspiration. The functions of Roman structures were also adapted by subsequent generations.

Ancient classic Greek architecture—aside from its stone block and column architecture (see page 20)—

[32] Production of a Roman solid poured cement form by means of a wooden mold. Reconstruction.

[33] Roman poured cement wall in Pompeii covered with tuff and bricks dating from the 1st century AD.

was characterized by rather insignificant and temporal wood and limestone structures. It was Roman invention that revolutionized not only the form and physical durability of buildings, but also the technical, organizational, and social aspects of construction, through innovations such as liquid concrete and baked bricks. Similar to the cement used today, which is liquefied and can therefore take on almost any form within a wooden mold, the Roman *opus caementicium* was a building material that quickly hardened, was capable of withstanding almost any weight, and was virtually indestructible. The rather ugly gray mass could be either covered over decoratively with various brick facings, or plated with polished marble, travertine slabs, or tuff (32, 33). Both the technique of pouring concrete as well as the compact masonry of baked bricks considerably enlarged the architectural forms available to builders. Cement allowed for the organization of facades by means of niches, indentations, and vaulted apses. Rooms increased in size, because it was now possible to deck them with poured concrete, wide-spanned barrel vaults, or even domes that measured more than 130 feet in diameter—as seen in the Pantheon in Rome (34). Constructions buttressed by supporting columns led to the building of massive substructures or foundations that could take on the form of suspended constructions, and aqueducts could now span entire valleys. Together, liquefied cement and the new masonry technique enabled the Romans to reach hitherto unheard of heights in their buildings.

A revolution in the social aspects of building paralleled these technical innovations. Greek column and stone block architecture had required highly specialized craftsmanship and trades for the cutting, transport, final shaping, and placement of the heavy building elements. The new Roman building techniques, in contrast, allowed the quick production of an enormous volume of construction material that, of course, required some organizers and specialists—especially for the wooden constructions and the building of molds—but chiefly depended on an enormous number of unskilled workers who did not need any special competencies. Slaves could therefore be used in the construction industry in great numbers. In addition, unskilled daily laborers were utilized in the areas of transport, the production of concrete and bricks, and the mounting of wooden structures—a pattern of employment arrangements consistently found in the building industry under the Roman emperors.

[34] Construction of a Roman cement dome by means of a supporting scaffold. Sketched reconstruction.

Thermal baths, villas, and palaces: Roman luxury architecture

Even today, life in ancient Rome seems to reflect luxury and decadence. This image was propagated by depictions in ancient classical literature itself, as well as by later historical portrayals, scenes from plays and films, and even comic books such as the Asterix series. There is an undeniable element of truth in this cliché, but it is not an apt characterization of the Republican period of Roman history. Authors like Cato praised the simple rural life consisting of honest daily labor over that of idleness and self-indulgence. But in the course of its conquests and expansion into the Mediterranean regions in the 2nd century BC, Rome came face-to-face with the refined forms of luxury prevalent in the Greek-Hellenistic city-states and underwent a radical change in attitude, mirrored in its architecture. Augustus, the first Roman emperor, strikingly formulated this change, boasting that during his reign he had transformed Rome from a city of bricks into a city of marble.

[35] Far beyond the Italian peninsula, Roman cement, whether in the form of bridges or tunnels, was often a symbol of the ability to tame inhospitable natural conditions on the part of an all-conquering culture that desired to subjugate all to its will. The Pont du Gard aqueduct near Nîmes in southern France dates from the 1st century AD.

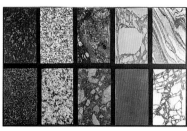

[36] A small selection of types of colored stones used in Roman buildings to cover cast cement structures.

Roman luxury in building first manifested itself in the materials used in construction. Marble of all hues and places of origin (36) was either employed structurally, as in columns or beams, or as a veneer for walls and ceilings made of brick or cast concrete. The more colorful the stone and the higher the quarrying price, the more grandiose the aura of the home or building—and the greater the renown of the spendthrift owner. The *cognoscenti* could not be fooled as to the difference between comparatively cheap white marble from the immediate vicinity (from the quarries of Carrara near Rome, for example) and the prestigious shimmering, finely grained marble from the Greek islands of Paros or Naxos. Connoisseurs deferred to the extremely expensive "real" red porphyr from Egypt. All the buildings which served to represent the grandeur of the state—that is, all public buildings having to do with state functions such as triumphal arches, theaters, and arsenals—were the recipients of such luxurious building materials. Often an inscription was placed in or near the building praising those who had commissioned it (for example, the city officials, the senate, the emperor, or private donors) and the expenses they had incurred.

[37] The Canopos, an artificial canal in the villa of the Roman emperor Hadrian in Tivoli (2nd century AD). The canal, lined with copies of Greek statues, led to a grotto rebuilt into a dining room.

A second category of opulence in Roman buildings can be found in those structures whose very function was anchored in luxury, particularly the Roman villa.

Although originally based on farm buildings in an agricultural milieu, during the 1st century BC, the villa developed more and more into the country seat of the urban upper class. The original design was thereby transformed into recreational architecture primarily devoted to the leisure of the owners. Villas of the 1st century AD formulated an entire world picture, including artificially created views that integrated nature into the buildings, grottos that were artificially hewn and then comfortably furnished, and burbling streams redirected to sprinkle "natural" gardens constructed with careful artifice. In addition, artfully gathered libraries and statue ensembles, mosaic decorations, and wall frescoes testified to the owners' emulation of Greek culture and learning—and, naturally enough, to the ambitions of the owner as well (37). The villa as the embodiment of a world of "natural" luxury posed an ideal that was to be imitated and carried forth into the Italian Renaissance and the Baroque architecture of Italy (see page 87). It would be only a small step from the magnificence of a villa to that of a palace for an emperor, governor, or—later—for a bishop. Already in the late classical age, villas and palaces were often similar in their architectural form as well as in their furnishings and interior design.

[38] The palace of the Roman emperor Diocletian in Split, built at the beginning of the 4th century AD: a luxurious architectural construction in the style of a military camp. Especially imposing in both design and decor was the seaward side with its docking area. Reconstruction drawing from 1912.

The large thermal baths in the cities, which can perhaps be considered the "palaces" of the people, were also an especially luxurious form of recreational architecture. Usually donations from the emperor or from communal magistrates, they were inevitably intended to manifest the largesse of the authorities. Admission to the baths was usually free of charge; male visitors could not only bathe but also take advantage of many other services: Doctors and dentists, fitness trainers, and lawyers had their quarters in the thermal baths, along with charlatans, quacks, and prostitutes. The buildings were of opulent dimensions and furnished with all imaginable comfort. Enormous glass windows lit up the elaborately decorated interiors with their domed or vaulted ceilings. A competent heating system provided cozy warmth, and expansive gardens and park grounds framed the buildings in which the urban population was induced to forget its otherwise rather modest standard of living.

"Natural" Architecture, Cave, and Earthen Structures

[39] The "primal hut" as a romanticized idealization of natural architecture: Frontispiece of the 2nd edition of Laugier's treatise, "Essay sur l'architecture," published in 1775.

Along with structures made of durable, permanent materials, there is also an ongoing tradition of so-called "natural" architecture embodying an almost endless multiplicity of forms and means. Natural architecture is either constructed of flimsy, nondurable materials or makes use of a natural formation, such as a cave formed into the earth or rock. Such works often result from a lack of economic means, a regional dearth of alternative building materials, or other external circumstances. In the mid 18th century, however, at the outset of the romantic age, Marc Antoine Laugier idealized these structures in his famous essay "Essay sur l'architecture" (Paris, 1753). But his visionary conception of a "primal cottage" (39) is a purely idealized invocation that is surely foreign to those actually living in such structures.

Cave architecture, which is usually considered an aspect of tomb architecture, has existed since antiquity. The most famous examples are undoubtedly the catacombs of Rome and Naples—burial sites, not originally of Christian character at all, that are laid out in labyrinthine subterranean passageways. Also of primary architectural significance are the Nabataean graves in Petra, Jordan, which are adorned with elaborate architectural facades (40).

Cave architecture has had a long tradition in many cultures throughout history. Mainly used in situations where there was a pressing need for defense, caves guaranteed almost complete protection against attack. The desire for effective defense is the motive behind the numerous rock churches found in Armenia, as well as for the extraordinarily large cave settlements found in Göreme, Turkey, and Matera, in southern Italy. These cities must once have appeared like mounds inhabited by thousands of termites. Today, while the Sassi of Matera, located in the inhospitable mountains of the Basilicata, are still used as dwellings, the rock caves of

Göreme have been transformed into tourist attractions.

The labyrinthine cave structures and fortified rock architecture found in China, Africa, North and South America, as well as Europe and Asia Minor, were used for protection and safety. There are, however, other kinds of "natural" constructions—analogous to the caves in their use of the natural resources at hand—made of more temporary building materials stemming from a completely different motive. Clay or mud constructions are a clear indication that other, more durable building materials are lacking; still, they often reflect the same architectural conceptions as structures built of more long-lasting wood or stone in other regions in the same time period. The old historical city of Sanaa, Yemen, for example, is a complete work of art sculpted in clay (43). The narrow, winding streets are lined with clay houses up to six stories high. Elaborately decorated on the exterior, these homes are

[40] Rock tomb in Petra, Jordan, 1st century AD. The enormous two-story relief facade reflects the Hellenistic-Greek influence in tomb structures.

[41]   Clay architecture of the Dogon tribe in the Arou area of Mali.

comfortable and above all cool on the inside.

The clay buildings of the Dogon people in today's Mali are equally artful, but are not as urban in their agglomeration (41, 42). Theirs are imaginative constructions, often roofed with bull-rush mats in a manner suggestive of the architectural expressionism of works by

[42]   Clay architecture of the Dogon tribe, Mali. A cross-section of the many rooms of the communal house of the extended Gindou family reveals the functionality of the multistory structure that was, in fact, planned as an entity.

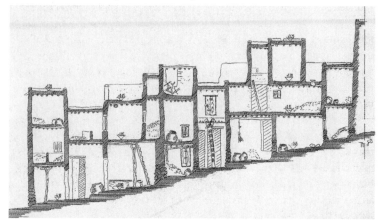

[43]   Clay buildings in Sanaa, Yemen.

Gaudí or Hundertwasser (see illus. 135, 148). Of course such buildings require continual care and repairs, but in return they offer both living and working quarters for the clans or extended families of up to 50 persons who inhabit them. The structure of the clay dwellings is usually rounded, with the rooms placed in rows, one on top of the other, like the chambers of a wasp's nest. Seen in cross-section, the buildings reveal an impressive, encompassing architectural structure which can rise to three stories in height (42).

Similar both in their impulse to use natural resources at hand and in the absence of any durable building materials are the leaf and wood huts of the Amazon Indians as well as the straw structures of various African tribes. The latter are longhouses, grouped together on one site; often enormous in size, only a few such structures are needed for an entire tribe. Here, as elsewhere, the living space and the uses it is put to reflect the society in which it originates. Depending on tribal customs, these longhouses can house a single family clan or various social groups distinguished according to their hierarchy within the tribe. Similar to these "primal huts" are the igloos of Alaskan and Greenland Indians, which serve as housing for extended families as well as defined groups in the social hierarchy. Although igloos are relatively small, they can be combined to form a labyrinthine conglomerate of adjoining structures, often of enormous size, with a similar social purpose.

[44] Prototype of an early Christian basilica: Agios Dimitrios in Thessalonica. Ground plans and reconstructed cross section of the five-aisled structure with anteroom (*narthex*), apse, and transept. Dating from the 5th century, the church has undergone numerous restorations and served as a mosque for several generations. The 20th-century restorations are based on the original building design.

Early Christian church architecture: Basilicas and central-plan buildings

The earliest Christian churches were built during the reign of Constantine, the first Roman emperor to convert to Christianity, in the 4th century AD. These early churches generally took the form of the basilica, an oblong building divided by rows of columns into three longitudinal aisles: a main vessel and two side aisles. The main vessel (in churches, later called the nave) of the basilica was a higher, two-story hall with windows on the upper level. On one of the narrower ends was a semi-circular apse with choir (44); the entrance was located on the opposite end, accompanied by an anteroom (*narthex*) and a cloistered court (*atrium*). This type of structure already enjoyed a long and varied functional tradition in ancient Roman architecture. In fact, the heterogeneity of the traditional

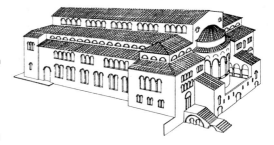

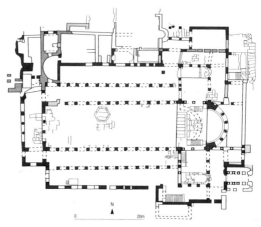

basilica was not always easy to reconcile with the aims of the new Christian cult. Initially basilicas had served as public buildings for vendors, traders, and legal officials. Situated adjacent to the forum in Roman cities, the building functioned as a kind of architectural annex to the plaza, and normally contained an entrance on the long side. The earliest Roman basilicas—the Porcia Basilica and the Opimia Basilica (2nd century BC) on the Forum Romanum—were named after their donors. Nonetheless, the actual origin of the basilica, whose name derives from the Greek word for "king," remains a matter of dispute.

Beginning in approximately AD 100, and increasingly in the late classical period, the basilica also became the favored part of stately villas and palaces. These long, multiple-aisled buildings, which were oriented toward the apse, served as the *aula regia*, the throne room or hall of state, for the rulers or patrons of a domain. The relationship between these profane pagan buildings and the early Christian basilicas remains a matter of debate. But already in the 4th century, it is clear that a structure similar to the basilica in Trier, initially conceived as the *aula regia* of Constantine's palace, was transformed into a Christian church. In the western Roman Empire—that is, Italy—a transept was commonly incorporated into the basilica in front of the apse or choir, thus giving the building the form of a cross and imparting unmistakable Christian character.

Although the basilicas in many of the early cities which adopted Christianity have fallen into ruin (see page 45), numerous early basilicas in Rome (among them, San Giovanni in Laterano, 4th century; Santa Sabina, 5th century) have survived, albeit in altered form or only through restoration. Historically, basilicas were often conceived as martyrs' shrines constructed above their graves after beatification. For this reason, basilicas were often situated on the site of an ancient necropolis, that is, outside of the ancient centers. These basilicas often became the foci of new Christian settlements.

bloody pogroms against the pagans
402
Removal of the western Roman court to Ravenna
482–511
Clovis founds Frankish realm
526
Death of Theoderic in Ravenna
527–567
Reign of Justinian; failed attempt to reunite the two Roman empires; consolidation of the Byzantine Empire
730
Beginning of iconoclasm after dissent over worship of images in religious ceremonies; reestablishment of iconography in 843
9th/10th centuries
Bulgaria and part of Russia fall under Byzantine influence; Saints Cyril and Methodius translate the Bible into the Slavic vernacular
1054
Great Schism between Eastern and Western churches
1186
Bulgaria breaks away from Byzantium; end of imperial Byzantine ambitions
1195
Byzantium pays tribute to German emperor Henry IV
1204
Conquest and plundering of Constantinople by Venetian troops during 4th crusade
1453
Sultan Mehmet conquers Constantinople; end of Byzantine Empire

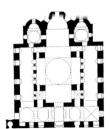

[45] The church Hagia Sophia in Thessalonica (8th century) is an early example of a multi-roomed, central-plan building. With an almost square foundation oriented toward a domed center, only the three apses indicate that the building was used for religious ceremonies.

[46] Panaghia Parigoritissa in Arta (western Greece), late 13th century. Building plan.

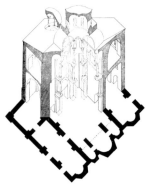

In the late 5th and 6th centuries, the development of the centrally organized or so-called central-plan building caused a striking transformation in church architecture. In contrast to the long, rectangular basilica organized along a single longitudinal axis, the central-plan building is based on two main axes of approximately the same length. The elements of the resulting structure are thus oriented not toward an apse at one end, but toward its own center. This type of centrally organized building also has a long tradition in Roman history, the most famous example in ancient Rome being the Pantheon, a round structure whose dome measures more than 130 feet in diameter, newly rebuilt in the 2nd century AD. Late classical mausoleums or funerary buildings were also central-plan structures, and many of these were transformed into churches during the 5th or 6th centuries, as for example, the Georgius rotunda, which originally functioned as the mausoleum of the Galerius palace in Thessalonica. Round buildings were not, however, the only ones susceptible to central organization. Square or polygonal structures (the mausoleum of Diocletian's palace in Split), as well as those in the form of a cross, could also be transformed into central-plan buildings. A central orientation could also develop from the basilica form, either through the combination of two basilicas into a cross built around a central point (San Vitale in Ravenna; Church of the Apostles in Istanbul), or through the merger of a long hall with a domed structure (Hagia Sophia in Istanbul; see page 41). At first, the central-plan design tended to comprise a single room, typically found in baptisteries (Hagia Eirene in Constantinople); but during the 8th century, the design was increasingly incorporated into major churches and parish churches in a multi-room format (45). By the middle to late Byzantine era, the central-plan building had developed into the predominant architectural form at the expense of the basilica.

The Panaghia Parigoritissa church in Arta (western Greece) is an architectural curiosity, but from the point of view of art history, its merger of Latin-Western and Byzantine-Eastern architectural forms represents a highly important central-plan

[47] Panaghia Parigoritissa in Arta (western Greece), late 13th century. View into the dome, which is supported by columns taken from another building and decorated with a mosaic of the omnipotent Christ.

structure. Constructed in 1290 on a nearly exactly square ground plan, the exterior of the church is reminiscent of a rustic Venetian *palazzo* (46, 47), but uncharacteristically sports a central dome that rises boldly on antique columns that were, in fact, removed from another site. Decorated with a mosaic of Christ the Almighty, the end result is a unique and daring structure, whose interior is impressively lit by means of various lanterns constructed into the roof. Other famous Byzantine central-plan buildings include the monastery churches of Daphni and Hosios Loukas in Greece, as well as more than 70 middle to late Byzantine churches or chapels. These buildings, with their great variety of central-plan designs (usually in a small format), seem to stand almost as though on exhibition in the city of Castoria, and can be found as well in the monasteries on the Athos peninsula (northern Greece). The central-plan design also developed into a standard to the north and the east, where Byzantine-Orthodox culture prevailed (including Russia, Bulgaria, and Serbia). In Western Europe, the central-plan building occured in direct response to specific political and religious situations, as exemplified by the Cathedral of St. Mark in Venice.

Building as experiment: The Hagia Sophia

The Hagia Sophia, or the Church of Holy Wisdom, in Istanbul was initially a prototype for the early Christian

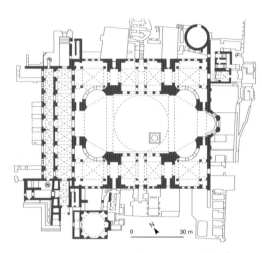

domed central-plan building (see page 39) and, later, for the domed mosque (see page 49). The Hagia Sophia possesses a highly eventful architectural history. An early church, probably in the form of a basilica, had already been constructed on the site about AD 360 under the Roman emperor Constantius II, but the structure was razed by fire in 404. A second basilica, built in 415, was completely destroyed during the Nika Revolt in 532.

Emperor Justinian (reigned from 527–565) personally initiated the reconstruction of a third church on the same site. Intended to be the coronation church of the East Roman-Byzantine emperors, it was intended to eclipse all other buildings in its magnificence. Between 532 and 537 the first building arose, an enormous construction that for the first time combined the form of the long, rectangular basilica with a central dome. The names of the architects have been passed down through history: Anthemios of Tralles and Isodoros of Milet, both cities in Asia Minor. The climax of the building was the daringly constructed dome. Resting on four massive columns anchored in rock beneath the foundation, the apex of the vault climbed to a height of more than 180 feet above the floor, and the diameter spanned almost 100 feet—an impressive distance, but still a good 45 feet short of the diameter of the Roman Pantheon.

The church, decorated with non-iconic mosaics reflecting the taste of the age, was consecrated in a magnificent ceremony on the 27th of December in 537 in the presence of the Emperor Justinian and Empress

Theodora. But the structure was not destined for a long life: In the summer of 558, the dome collapsed. In contradiction to popular belief, the disaster was probably not a result of damage possibly incurred during a weak earthquake in 557, but rather seems to have been a not uncommon occurrence intrinsically rooted in ancient and medieval building techniques. In those days, the mathematical basis of structural engineering—a matter taken for granted today—was still more or less unknown; the technical limits of architectural structures were discovered through a process of trial and error. As a result, many Gothic cathedrals also collapsed (see page 79). Not precise calculation, but time alone, indicated which buildings would succeed and which would fail, that is, literally collapse. In fact, the collapse of a building was a far more common event than is generally imagined today, but only in spectacular cases, as that of the Hagia Sophia, was public attention aroused.

The specific reason for the catastrophe of the Hagia Sophia probably resided in the shallowness of the curve of the dome. At least, this is what the design of the replacement dome seems to suggest. With its diameter of 108 feet, the new dome deviated from a circular outline, rising an additional 23 feet in height. Built between 558 and 563 by Isodoros the Younger, presumably the son of the first architect, the dome was also supported by a stronger load-bearing construction. Along the longitudinal axis, the entire structure is further supported by two semi-domes, which lend additional stability to the whole. These oddities and irregularities are visible neither from the interior nor the exterior; architecturally, the church gives the visitor an impression of complete harmony. At the second consecration

[48] Left page: Hagia Sophia. Ground plan of the complex with the renovations and alterations undertaken (558–563) after the collapse of the dome in 558.

[49] Not only the dome of the Hagia Sophia was an architectural masterpiece. The magnificent windows, which flooded the interior with natural light, were also a triumph of structural engineering.

The question of whether the advent of Christianity implied a complete rejection of the ancient pagan world in favor of Christian-Western ideals—a true change of epochs—is one of history's vexed questions. Often colored with ideological or dogmatic interest, it cannot be answered with a simple yes or no. Despite various setbacks, for instance the neo-pagan "reforms" of the emperor Julian the Apostate (reigned 361–363), Christianity steadily gained ascendancy over the gods of the ancient world after the conversion of Emperor Constantine (reigned 324–337). By the end of the 5th century, radical Christian rulers such as the emperors Theodosius (reigned 379–395) and Justinian (reigned 527–565) ensured the irreversibility of not only a spiritual and religious transition, but also a more fundamental social and economic one. From the historical perspective, this transformation was less an abrupt break than a gradual process, and thus not an epochal change.

On the other hand, inspection of the early Christian building monuments considerably qualifies this conciliatory view. Although the architecture of the classic and Christian eras flows together on a continuum through the repeated transformation of temples into churches, the buildings and monuments of the early Christian era nevertheless must be seen as belonging to the classical world. Many once-splendid complexes, especially those on Greek soil, fell into ruins between the 5th and 8th centuries and have not survived; thus, in both a physical sense and in an antiquarian sense these earliest structures more resemble the pagan shrines of Delphi or Olympia, and have nothing to do with Christianity as it exists today. The ruins are important to art history, but express nothing of an essentially "Christian" worldview.

Nicopolis ("Victory City"), founded in northwestern Greece by the emperor Augustus in 27 BC after his naval victory at nearby Actium, became an important Christian center during the reign of the East Roman emperor Justinian in the 6th century. Splendid basilicas decorated with marble plates and mosaics, complemented by bishop's palaces and baptisteries, sprouted up in the city. This area of concentration was girded by a new city wall that radically reduced the size of the new Christian "city" in comparison with the old settlement. The area, barely 1,300 ft. on each side, had more the

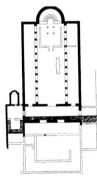

[50] Ground plan of Basilica A in Amphipolis in northern Greece, 5th century. In front of the three-aisled basilica was an atrium, a colonnaded courtyard of nearly square dimensions.

air of a monastery than of a vital settlement, literally becoming a labyrinthine "church city" of interconnected Christian spiritual buildings. In the course of the tribal migrations of the early Middle Ages, the area fell into ruins. A new, now Byzantine-Christian, center grew up in nearby Arta (ancient city of Ambrakia), whose famed ecclesiastical buildings are still a popular tourist destination today (see illus. 40).

The testimony offered by the northern Greek cities of Amphipolis and Philippi is very similar. During the late classical period they were transformed from prominent pagan settlements into palatial church cities. The churches in their centers were veritable treasures but, as in Nicopolis, they fell into ruins in the late 7th century. At its height in the 5th century, Amphipolis contained five basilicas, richly decorated with mosaics, reliefs, and marble plating (50). Of considerable dimensions, they were built so close together that they were structurally integrated with one another in places. Philippi, famous in Christianity as the city visited by the Apostle Paul in AD 49, also contained expansive basilica buildings constructed around 500. They were partly connected with an enormous bishop's palace, an image of worldly splendor in a Christian-ecclesiastical context. The ruins of Basilica B (51) still convey a sense of the size and opulence of these late classic church buildings. There were

numerous Christian "church cities" dating from the same era on the southern Balkan peninsula, which also deteriorated during the 7th–8th centuries. Of particular importance were Nea Anchialos, the "Phtiotic" Thebes by the Gulf of Volos in central Greece, and the late classical settlement near Stobi in what is now Macedonia. These "church cities" of numerous basilicas, baptisteries, and bishop's palaces lack a tradition of continuous settlement into modern times; they are in fact the ruined cities of early Christendom.

[51] The ruins of Basilica B in Philippi, 6th century. The colonnade of colored marble columns with chiseled capitals in the interior of the church still conveys an impression of the church's former magnificence.

In most histories of art and architecture, "Byzantine architecture" denotes almost exclusively ecclesiastical buildings. While churches are indisputably the crowning jewels of Byzantine building, they were not the sole achievements of this rich period. For many humanistic archaeologists and art historians, buildings located on ancient sites were simply obstacles to recovery of the prized ancient ruins. As late as the 1960s, Byzantine constructions were razed during excavations, often without documentation, and with them their historical witness. The emphasis of architectural knowledge of the period on Byzantine churches is not the result of chance, but of these ignorant acts of destruction.

[52] The Byzantine city wall of Constantinople. Reconstructed drawing by archaeologist F. Krischen.

of the building, once again in the presence of the court, the poet Paulos Silentiarios composed a panegyric on Justinian, his regency, and the magnificence of the new church. The document is of great importance today in providing a picture of the Hagia Sophia in the 6th century, for it describes the original interior decoration that has since been lost through repeated renovation. When the Ottomans under Mehmet II conquered the city of Constantinople on May 29, 1453, the Hagia Sophia was reconsecrated as the city's central mosque. Somewhat later the four minarets, which are still so striking today, were added.

Byzantine fortifications and settlements

The architecture of Byzantine settlements, especially those of the capital of the empire, were in a sense the continuation of classic Roman architectural tradition. Pragmatic and technical matters were of greater concern than aesthetic aspects. One real marvel of military construction was the city wall of Byzantium (52). In front of a chain of recessed fortified towers stood a massive wall, studded with small bastions in the form of protruding bays in the facade, and a wide moat. The city's harbors could even be closed off with massive chains to discourage unwanted intruders from the sea. An elaborate system of water pipes and fountains throughout the city attest to the direct continuation of the technical achievements of the *Imperium Romanum*—as do the architectural luxury of structural ornamentation on building segments such as capitals, the bases of columns, marble-plated walls, and the various forms of adornment found on external walls (53).

The ruins of Mistra near Sparta, Greece, offer a good view of the architecture of a self-contained Byzantine domestic settlement. From the early 14th century, Mistra, especially famous for its silk industry, was the Byzantine center of the Peloponnese, functioning in a sense as capital, royal residence, and monastic

center all in one. The city itself was broadly laid out on a slope in an easily defensible position. Numerous narrow streets lined with houses wound up the side of the hill; above them towered the massive, walled fortress that had been built by Frankish desperadoes in the 13th century and had later been taken over by the Byzantines. In the 15th century, Mistra was first conquered by the Ottomans and then by different Western-Latin troops. Finally, however, during the Greek war of independence in the early 19th century, Mistra fell completely into ruins. Only the churches and monasteries with their monumental museum-like character have survived in good condition, although almost no traces remain of the housing or fortifications. The palace (54), situated halfway up the slope, is an exception. It has been nearly completely reconstructed and is considered the most famous example of Byzantine palace architecture today.

A striking testimony to the Byzantine presence, especially in Greece, are the fortresses built largely during the early Middle Ages on top of ancient ruins. Many old Greek cities, especially in the western and central peninsula, had been refounded or moved to hill tops or other elevations that could more easily be defended during the uneasy times of the 3rd and 2nd centuries BC. Later, the Byzantines, profiting from these ancient ruins, made use of the same locations for their castles and fortresses. Thus, during the 8th to 10th centuries AD, fortified citadels arose like a row of fangs on top of ancient ruins. Although resting one on top of the other, the different masonry techniques make the various historical layers clearly visible even to the unpracticed eye: at base, the ancient Greek foundation is built of massive stone blocks structured polygonally or in staggered layers; on top is a simple and quickly erected Byzantine rubble wall structure.

[53] Byzantine ornamentation: Detail from the external side of the choir-apse of the Pantanassa Monastery in Mistra, Greece, early 15th century.

[54] The despot's palace in Mistra, Greece. Reconstruction of the wing containing the throne room and a loggia on the lower level.

The mosque: An architectural structure with a past

The classical world had provided fertile humus for both the Roman papal tradition of the West and the Byzantine Orthodox one of the East. In the early 7th century a third cultural subsystem arose, the roots of which also reached back, at least in part, to the ancient classical world. Islam, like Christianity, is a monotheistic religion with a specific religious founder (Mohammed). At first Islam was confined to the Arabian peninsula (Mecca and Medina), but it expanded rapidly in the 8th century. As in the two early Christian spheres of influence, sacred buildings were also dominant in the Islamic culture—but now in the form of the mosque.

The ceremonial requisites of Islam were at first quite simple. As a result, both the forms of the mosques, and the uses they were put to, varied considerably. Aside from their function as the locus of religious worship, mosques also served as secular centers for the community. At the core of all mosques was a prayer room precisely oriented toward Mecca on its longitudinal axis; directly opposite the entrance was the apse-formed prayer niche, or *mihrab*, facing toward Mecca. To the right of the niche was the pulpit (*mimbar, mirbar*). Another essential feature was the *minaret* (55), at first a rather squat structure but later a sleek lance-like tower, from which the *muezzin* called the believers to prayer. In its structural foundation, the mosque is similar to early Christian churches (see page 38) with a main building, oriented axially, enclosed in a courtyard with a splendid entrance portal.

Within this basic concept, however, significant regional differences developed. In the Arabic lands of North Africa and later in the regions of Europe they conquered, a flat-roofed prayer room designed like a multi-naved basilica with a long rectangular courtyard in front predominated. In the mosques of Central Asia and the Indian subcontinent, the courtyard became the center of the entire complex, and the prayer room, more of an annex, was greatly reduced in size. In the same region we find mainly square, and even dia-

The Architecture of Islam

gonally arranged, floor plans. Although similar in layout, the mosques of West Africa and the Sahel include a much larger prayer room. In western Africa as in Central Asia, the mosques share not only a basic structural concept; a recognizably regional style of design predominates in the formal details, ornamentation, and the building materials employed. The pavilion-mosques and stepped-roofed mosques of China and Southeast Asia (56) blend especially smoothly into the indigenous architecture customary to the religious buildings and shrines of Buddhism. Mosques are, in fact, often only recognizable by their minarets.

The type of structure that visitors to Turkey today assume is the norm of the "mosque" is actually a more recent development than the mosques of northern Africa and Central Asia. The structure of the "typical" Turkish-style mosque is specifically related to the basic plan of the Byzantine church. Probably inspired by the Hagia Sophia in Istanbul, which was transformed from a church into a mosque in the 15th century and substantially expanded, this type of mosque is mainly found in Asia Minor and Anatolia. The classic example is the so-called Blue Mosque in Istanbul (57), with its sea of domes and six slender minarets visible from afar. Dating from the early 17th century, the Blue Mosque consists of a domed, nearly square central building with an adjacent arcaded courtyard—also square and nearly identical in dimension to the floor plan of the central building. The wide, expansive dome stretching across the entire space was an early feature of mosques, linking Islamic architecture equally to the Judaic-Christian tradition and to ancient Rome. Dating from the 1st century AD, the Roman Pantheon offered not only the technical inspiration for future domed constructions, but also established the dome symbolically as a cosmic, all-

[55] The Spiral Minaret of the mosque of Samarra (Iraq), dating from the mid-9th century, is a prominent feature of what was at the time the world's largest mosque, with space for 100,000 believers. Rising more than 180 ft. above the ground, the tower is strikingly different from the slender, needle-formed minarets of later years.

[56] Sketch of a building plan for a mosque in Southeast Asia. The stepped roof of the central building is reminiscent of a pagoda; only the tower (minaret), standing somewhat in isolation, reveals the building's function as a mosque.

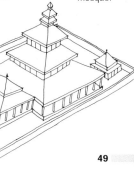

[57] The Blue Mosque in Istanbul, built by Sedefkar Mehmet Aga under commission from the Sultan Ahmet, about 1610. The building acquired its name from the patterned blue painting of its tile work and the blue calligraphy in the interior.

encompassing image of heaven. The oldest domed central-plan building of Islam is Dome of the Rock in Jerusalem, dating from the late 7th century (58).

Both inside and out, mosques were richly ornamented with colorful decorations. The splendid colors of the Dome of the Rock—the gleaming golden dome, the blue-white base, and the minute ornamentation executed in many different techniques—are not at all unusual. In the interior, what often seems to the "non-believer" to be an especially beautiful ornament proves on closer inspection to be much more: Painted calligraphy presenting *suras* (verses) from the Koran in Arabic adorn the interior of buildings so fully and so pictorially that those unacquainted with the script often mistake these letters for a beautiful decoration and fail to recognize the Koran texts used in religious ceremonies.

Today, in practically all Islamic nations, the construction of mosques is still one of the vital tasks of architecture. Many spectacular mosques arose in the 20th century, although only a few—such as the Bhong mosque in the Pakistani province of Punjab, completed in 1982—are done in the highly elaborate, historically oriented style. Ironically enough, during the most religiously conservative, Shi'ite-fundamentalist period of its history, Iran created the prototype for the modern mosque: The al-Ghadir mosque in Teheran is considered the most important monument of modern Islamic architecture.

Sinan, court architect to Suleyman the Magnificent

Probably born in 1497 in Cappadocia, Sinan was a non-Turkish Christian forcibly impressed into the elite janissary troops of Sultan Suleyman the Magnificent in

1512, and thereby converted to Islam. Sinan's unusual career catapulted him to become the most prominent architect in the history of Islamic architecture. A trained carpenter, Sinan accompanied the military campaigns of the sultan as an engineer and architect beginning in 1520. His simple, readily-built military constructions for siege or defense were works of genius, but it was his inventiveness in the construction of new tools and equipment that soon raised him from the anonymous ranks of Islamic architects and engineers. In 1530, while still in military service, Sinan was given his first commissions for religious buildings. Upon finishing military service in 1538, Sinan assumed responsibility for public and religious architecture, remaining active at the court of the sultan in Istanbul until his death in 1588.

One narrative—at times an ornate, fairy-tale like story, fashioned after his death by an unknown hand—recounts Sinan's deeds, listing 477 buildings supposedly erected under his direction, including 157 mosques, 74 *madrasahs* or Koran schools, 56 baths, 45 magnificent tombs, 38 palaces and 31 caravansaries, in addition to hospitals, libraries, bridges, and other works relating to the infrastructure, such as redesigning the water supply system for Istanbul. In terms of architectural history, Sinan is primarily known for his complete modernization of mosque construction. His goal was to optimize the design of the buildings and surpass aesthetically everything done up to that point. For Sinan, however, optimizing design did not mean surpassing an already-existing masterpiece in a larger physical form; instead, he ascribed to the Asian tradition and its conception of art. Sinan's main interest was vaulted architecture, and so he

[58] The intersection of cultures and one of the earliest monuments of Islam: The Dome of the Rock, a richly decorated, domed octagon in Jerusalem, was begun under Caliph Abd al-Malik around 690.

concentrated his attention on the idea of the domed mosque, which had come to be integral to the concept of the Ottoman mosque of the 14th century. Thus, the enormous dome of the Hagia Sophia in Istanbul, which had been built in the 7th century, remained for Sinan the measure for his own works. He did not wish to outdo the building or its dome in terms of size; rather, his goal was an ever-varying repetition of optimal components, an achievement that for him was embodied in minutely calculated ideal proportions, in an aesthetically satisfying arrangement of differently dimensioned vaulted rooms around a center, and in the harmonious connection between external and interior views. Sinan's conception of the optimum explains the large number of mosques he erected: At first glance they seem identical, but in actuality no two are alike.

Of the 477 buildings literary sources attribute to Sinan, the majority have not survived. Looking back on his life in the 1580s, Sinan himself mentioned three of his works as especially significant. He termed the Prince Mosque in Istanbul (built 1542–1548) his "apprentice piece." A high central building flanked by two minarets, its large central dome is surrounded by a sea of smaller subsidiary domes, its details presaging the later design of the Blue Mosque (see illus. 57).

[59] The large, well-lit domed hall of the Suleyman mosque in Istanbul is comparable in design to the central hall of the Hagia Sophia (see illus. 48, 49).

He considered the mosque commissioned by Sultan Suleyman (built 1550–1557), also in Istanbul, his "journeyman's piece." Its enormous domed central hall is based on the Hagia Sophia, and his design emphasizes a sense of spaciousness in the interior (59). Sinan's true masterpiece, in his own opinion, was the mosque for Sultan Selim II in Edirne (built 1568–1574; 60).

Islam on the offensive: Alhambra and the Taj Mahal

The expansion of Islam—simultaneously with its development from a regional

Arabic to a world culture—took place under the Omayyad dynasty (661–750), centered in Damascus. Like wildfire, the Arabian religion and way of life spread first through North Africa; from there, campaigns were launched toward Sicily and the Iberian peninsula in an attempt to conquer even Western Europe. In Sicily, Arab invasions constituted but a short intermezzo, whereas in Spain the effort was successful over the longer term. In AD 711 the "Saracen storm" crossed the Strait of Gibraltar. For the next 800 years large parts of southern Spain became a bastion of Islam. Only in 1492 was the *reconquista*, or reconquering, of this important part of the European mainland achieved by Christian armies.

[60] The mosque built for Sultan Selim II in Edirne. Sinan was given free reign not only over its architectural design, but also its ornamentation.

One result of this territorial expansion was the spread of the Islamic architectural canon. If interest at first focused primarily on the mosque, later a wide spectrum of architectural forms, sacred as well as profane, developed under the Omayyad dynasty including *madrasahs* (Koran schools), residences and palaces, public buildings like bath houses, and infrastructural projects like streets, bridges, or the system of fountains. Wealth and luxury became characteristic, even proverbial, of Oriental life. Rulers' buildings were fitted especially richly with colorful ornamentation, partly as reliefs and partly applied; interiors were no less opulently decorated and furnished with costly materials.

The prototype of Islamic palace architecture is the Alhambra near Granada, Spain (61). Erected between 1238 and 1358 on a low but easily defensible elevation, the enormous complex—almost a small, fortified city encircled within a wall—is far more than a single palace. The heart of the complex was an abandoned 11th-century castle. The Nasrid rulers resided in the Alhambra, with the rule of Yussuf I (1333–1354) being of exceptional magnificence and importance.

Structurally, the Alhambra is reminiscent of a medieval fortress expanded into a castle (see page 73). A 3-foot-thick wall, armed with battlements, encloses the complex. Within these confines, the complex is divided into various palace sections along the longitudinal axis. Behind the entrance, the visitor progresses first through two garden-like courtyards before arriving at the first building (for servants), positioned perpendicularly to the axis. Passing through a narrow passageway, the visitor enters another large courtyard positioned behind the first, again perpendicularly. At the center of the court is a water fountain, and on the narrow side, a massive tower structure (the "Hall of Messengers"). Only at this point, reached by means of winding paths, does the actual residential area begin: An almost square peristyle complex with stately halls and living areas grouped around a courtyard. What distinguished the Alhambra from other late medieval castle and fortress complexes was its exceptional luxury, the magnificence of its buildings. Situated in an area of little to no rainfall, the entire complex is still endowed with gardens containing many pools. The slender, columned walkways are decorated lavishly with pointed arches and ornamental plasterwork, and an artfully sculptured fountain, whose basin rests on the backs of 16 lions, graces the palace's central courtyard.

Like the Alhambra in the west, the Taj Mahal (62) is the architectural icon of Islam in the East—an architectural wonder seemingly sprung from one of the tales of the Thousand and One Nights. In the course of Islam's eastward expansion, elements of the northern Indian Islamic religion merged with the Moghul Dynasty in power during the 11th and 12th centuries. Under Shah Jahan (reigned 1628–1658), the Taj Mahal was built on

[61] The Alhambra near Granada. Ground plan of the castle and park grounds.

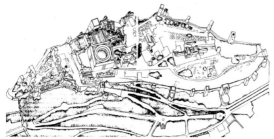

the south bank of the Jumna River near the city of Agra, India, as an elaborate tomb, but also an over-whelming monument to Jahan's own reign and the economic potency of his dynasty. The gleaming white central-plan building arises out of the wide plains in incomparable majesty, a unique testimony to the homogeneity of Islamic architecture. The building is given its contour by a square plinth, or base, at whose four corners slender minarets are positioned. The onion-shaped dome, visible only from the outside (in the interior the dome has been disguised), crowns the central building and is again surrounded by four small octagonal towers. The central dome itself measures almost 92 feet in diameter and 213 feet high from the floor. On each of the four sides, an oblong room about 66 feet deep with a richly ornamented facade opens. The interior is organized around the tomb chamber, which was open to pilgrims. Through skillful structural arrangements, the masses of visitors are channeled and led in a kind of procession past the monument to the dead.

Set into a long rectangular landscape enclosed by a wall, the mausoleum itself is only a small part of the entire park-like complex. A monumental entrance portal of reddish sandstone contrasts strikingly with the white marble of the mausoleum itself, marking the entrance to a park that is designed like a kind of cloister. Two intersecting water channels, laid out on a rigid axis, lead through the garden up to the mauso-leum. Only the last quarter of the area is designed architectonically: This area is occupied by the mauso-leum itself as well as by two smaller buildings, the mosque and the resting house flanking the mauso-leum. The Taj Mahal was originally intended to be the burial site for Jahan's beloved wife. He also planned a complementary building nearby for himself, made of black stone. But, overthrown by his son in 1658, the Shah could not realize this dream; after his death in 1666 he was buried next to his favorite wife in the Taj Mahal.

[62]   The Taj Mahal, erected between 1630 and 1653. The architect of the building is un-known; the structure is stylistically a mixture of Indian Mogul architec-ture, Timuridic mauso-leums, and Persian-Safawidic decorative elements.

Monasteries, stupas, and pagodas: The religious architecture of Buddhism

The architecture of the East Asian cultures is fundamentally heterogeneous, bearing the stamp of regional characteristics as well as that of the various religious practices of the three great eastern religions: Buddhism, Hinduism, and Shintoism. An entire book would be necessary to expound the multiplicity of the various architectural forms. Perhaps for this reason, surveys of architecture often completely ignore this complex, multi-faceted chapter of architectural history and focus their perspective on the western world alone. What follows provides at least a basic outline of eastern architecture with some of its essential features.

The stupa, the simplest form of the religious monument in Buddhism, was at first a simple construction of wood and earth, intended to house relics. The hemispherical structure—later bell-shaped—built upon a round base originally functioned as a burial mound for important personages. Early on, however, the function of the stupa took on a purely religious significance. Composed of a massive mound of earth (which was soon found to be more durable if reinforced by a covering of stones), the stupa is topped by a mast with a number of overlapping umbrellas. The oldest examples of the stupa date back to the 5th–3rd centuries BC (63). With the expansion of Buddhism through the Southeast Asian mainland to Ceylon, Indonesia and Java, Korea, and China, the stupa form spread, spatially as well as temporally, resulting

[63]   The stupa in Svayambhunath, Nepal, is the oldest Buddhist shrine in the region. Through the centuries it has been remodelled so often, that it is not possible to determine an exact date. It probably dates from the 5th century AD.

in significant regional changes that are apparent, for instance, in the pyramid-like structures on Java and Bali. The single most important stupa of Buddhism is the so-called Golden Pagoda, the Shwe Dagon Pagoda in Rangoon, Burma. Begun in 1372 on the site of a previous structure (erected, according to legend, in 468 BC over the relic of 8 hairs from the Buddha's beard), its silhouette is somewhat reminiscent of an inverted funnel.

Another variant of the stupa is the classically formed and proportioned pagoda, which soon took on an independent existence. The pagoda is an upward-striving structure constructed on a square or polygonal (or, rarely, on a round) ground plan (65). The high, soaring body of the building is based on the stupa form, but the artfully crafted, projecting roofs curving upward above each story are borrowed from the saddle-like hipped roofs used to cover native halls, particularly in China. These structures, which consist of only one story inside, appear from the outside to have two stories because of the narrowing of the lean-to roof. Beginning in the 2nd century AD, they became the primary religious structures of temple and shrine enclaves. Later, as an architectural form robbed of its religious-ceremonial function but imbued with the exotic flair of something typically "Chinese," the pagoda graced park and garden landscapes in many European cities during the 18th and 19th centuries.

Various Buddhist temple forms resembling a stepped pyramid (found in Thailand, for example) are also considered variants of stupa architecture. In addition to these explicitly religious buildings, Buddhist architecture includes numerous buildings: palaces and monasteries, communal buildings for monks, as well as stately rooms and defensive structures pertaining to the secular world. Numerous examples of Buddhist monastery and palace complexes with their characteristic multi-storied form that turns a cold-shoulder to the outside world can be found in the inhospitable moun-

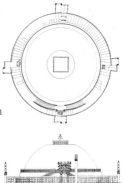

[64] Stupa of Sanchi, India, 5th century BC. Foundation and reconstructed cross section.

[65] Five-story pagoda of Khumbheshvara, a Shiva sanctionary, in Lalithpur, Kathmandu, in Nepal.

tainous world of the Himalayas, in Nepal, or Tibet. One
prominent example is the Potala Palace in Lhasa, built
in the 17th century under the fifth Dalai Lama, which is
a mixture of palace, defensive fortress, and monastery.

Angkor: Jungle complex in Cambodia

With the erection of the temple complex Angkor (66)
at the beginning of the reign of King Yashovarman I
(reigned 889–910), the Khmer Empire reached the
height of its political influence. Conquered by the
armies of the Tai state in 1431 and then gradually abandoned, the complex sank back into the lush vegetation
of the jungle. Situated about 140 miles northwest of
Phnom Penh, far from all modern routes of transportation, Angkor was rediscovered by the Frenchman
Henri Mouhot in 1860 while he was carrying out a
land survey for the colonial power. His find was one of
the great archaeological sensations of the 19th century.

The newly discovered capital was a highly artificial
formation, completely planned down to the last details.
Originally, the complex was laid out on an exact square
and was meant to function as a symbol of the entire
world. At its center was an enormous temple mountain, an analogue to the world-mountain Meru that
figures in the Indian Brahman cosmology. A gigantic
system of rectangular artificial lakes or reservoirs
formed the economic and political power basis of the
complex and provided a system of irrigation for intensive rice cultivation. Three harvests a year could be
garnered, bringing immense riches to the inhabitants
as well as the ruling dynasty residing there. The econo-

[66] Angkor, in the
Cambodian jungle.

mic situation in turn determined the cityscape: Based on evidence offered by the ruins, there appear to have been numerous storage buildings at the periphery of the settlement. However, determining the function of buildings outside the center is problematic. Because the complex was sacred, numerous Hindu-Brahman temples were scattered throughout the area, making it unclear whether a larger population lived here at all. Various additions and renovations altered its once symmetrical character, especially the area added around 1200 called Angkor Thom, walled off from the rest, a kind of complex within the complex.

[67] Figure from the temple-mausoleum Angkor Wat, lavishly decorated with reliefs and sculptures, 12th century.

In terms of architectural history and the history of art, the zenith of Angkor is Angkor Wat (66, 67), a funerary temple built by King Suryavarman II (reigned 1113–1150) in the southern part of the city center. The mausoleum was meant to ensure the immortality of the king and to celebrate the Vishnu cult, highly important to Brahmanism. The building rises up on a rectangular base demarcated by a water ditch (today dry) that is almost 875 ft. wide and 4,921 x 4,165 ft. on each side. The central building consists of a three-stepped pyramid, whose levels are surrounded by galleries marked by corner towers and, at the center, a fifth tower, rising above the others. The core building is ringed by an external and an inner wall, also complete with corner towers. A wide, absolutely straight road led through a magnificent portal to the entrance. The complex is richly sculpted (67), with particular significance attached to a complexly staggered low-relief frieze that graces more than 1,600 ft. of the length of an interior gallery in the core building.

Sacred architecture of Hinduism and Shinto

In contrast to Buddhism, Hinduism is not tied to any founder. Arising from Brahmanism in the 2nd century BC, this religion conceives of itself as an eternal, absolute world law (*dharma*) that allows the individual considerable freedom as to the form her or his faith takes. Concretely, Hinduism has an almost incomprehensible number of gods, and thereby takes on the traits of polytheism. Well into the 12th century, Hinduism had difficulties making headway against Buddhism on the Indian subcontinent, but afterward it became the dominant religion of this region (India, Pakistan, Sri Lanka) as well as some neighboring areas (Brahmanism of the Khmer culture, see page 60). Prayer and offerings in the temple are at the heart of Hinduism, and accordingly, temple structures are the earliest and most characteristic of Hinduism's architectural heritage. Hindu temple complexes are highly symbolic structures that hardly look like buildings at all, but more like enormous sculpted or modeled formations. All of the temples present an eternal and omnipresent symbolic visualization of the holy mountain Meru. They rise up on a high base which is reached by way of a steep, exterior flight of stairs.

Khajuraho in India is a significant site of early Hindu temple architecture. During the regency of the Candella dynasty (9th century AD), numerous temples arose which—like the Khmer city of Angkor—fell into ruins during the 12th century. They were swallowed by the jungle, only to be rediscovered at the beginning of the 20th century. The most significant building was the well-preserved Kanarya Mahadeva (Kandariya Mahaheo) temple, erected about the year 1000. Its oblong building plan (68) in the style of a double central-plan building reveals an inner ambulatory connecting the two centers with each other: the Mandapa hall and the sanctuary beneath the large Sikhara tower. Rising up from a high base, the building is of soft, light-colored sandstone and lavishly decorated. Characteristic of this structure along with all other Hindu temples is a wealth of figural relief sculpture and architectural ornamentation full of fantasy, much like fretwork in stone or ivory carvings. They form a striking contrast to the comparative dearth of ornamentation on the Buddhist stupa.

[68] Kanarya Mahadeva Temple, Khajuraho, India, about 1000. Cross section.

Shinto, the predominant religion in Japan, arose in prehistoric times and is imbued with shamanistic ideas: Honoring nature and one's ancestors are the two cornerstones of this religion. Its ceremonies invoke the *kami*, the nature or ancestor spirits, who are worshipped at shrines, light wooden structures forming the center of a holy district. High wooden fences surround the shrine, hiding it from inquisitive gazes from without, but one may enter through a wooden door (*torii*), usually painted red. A shrine is always situated along running water for the cleansing rituals. The oldest intact Shinto shrine is the Izumo shrine on the island Honshu, also called the Ise shrine (70). Founded in the 2nd century AD, the shrine as it exists today no longer dates from this period. As a rule, since the year 690, Shinto shrines have been torn down and rebuilt in identical form approximately every 20 years, so that today's shrine is a modern execution. The form, however, especially that of the continuous roof molding, is an exact replica of that from the 2nd century AD. In this way, architectural tradition has continued through the ages perfectly. Shinto shrines are thus new buildings and ancient pieces of architecture at the same time.

With the intrusion of Chinese culture into Japan from the 6th century, diverse Buddhist architectural patterns found footing, particularly the multistoried pagoda and the halls with their tetrahedral, hip, or saddle roofs scrolled upward at the corners. A specialty of traditional Japanese architecture is an exceptionally light building method, even outside of sacred architecture: filigree wooden constructions with light walls of thin boards, movable screens, or even frames of paper. A perfect example of this style is the emperor's palace in Kyoto, reconstructed in the 19th century from old etchings and notations. Similar principles were often observed by Japanese garden architecture, such as tea houses.

[69] Kanarya Mahadeva Temple, Khajuraho, India, about 1000. The base of the temple consists of sandstone abundantly decorated with figures and ornamentation which render the building itself a work of sculpture.

[70] The Ise shrine on the island of Honshu, Japan: a seemingly modern building dating from the 1980s, but adhering exactly to the form of a religious building dating from about AD 200.

Pyramids, temples and settlements of the Aztecs and Incas

Beginning around 2500 BC, a number of advanced civilizations arose in the vast area stretching between central South America and northern Mexico. The diversity of these pre-Columbian cultures makes it extremely difficult to treat them as a unit; the only common denominator is their dramatic demise in the course of the European conquests of the 16th century. In popular opinion, the Maya, Aztecs, and Incas appear as almost the sole exemplars of ancient American culture, but in fact they were only a small, if important, part of a highly complex ethnic constella-tion in this area. Moreover, the Aztec and Incan cultures are quite recent phenomena: The Aztecs were a nomadic people who migrated into Mexico around AD 1300 and became sedentary. Similarly, the Inca kingdom in the heights of the Andes (in today's Peru) arose around the year 1200. Only the Mayan culture, which stretched through Central America from the Yucatan peninsula across the territory covered by the present-day countries of Belize, Honduras, and Guatemala, possessed deep historic roots. The earliest archaeological traces of the Mayans reach back to approximately 2500 BC.

The dominant architectural form in the Mayan and Aztec empires was the pyramid. These structures are not to be confused with the Egyptian pyramids dating from the age of the pharaohs (see page 11). The Mesoamerican pyramids were terraced and could be climbed by means of stairs. Furthermore, with a few exceptions, the pyramids served not as the tombs for rulers, but as artificial mountains whose uppermost platforms were the site of extensive temple complexes. By far the largest such structure in Mesoamerica is the Sun Pyramid of Teotihuacán (71), set in the cen-tral Mexican highland. Built in the 3rd century AD, the pyramid rises 215 feet above the plain, measures 722 feet on end, and is constructed of 1.3 million cubic yards of air-dried bricks. Ramps and stairs lead to the top, which at one time was the site of religious worship. Similar structures are found in other places as well. There is great variation among the pyramids in terms of their basic forms, angles of inclination, and building techniques, according to the time period in which they were built, as

well as the region and culture in which they arose. Nonetheless, they all shared two elements: a podest-like structure and their purpose, namely, the religious rites performed on them. A few of the most significant pyramids are those of the Maya of Tikal (6th century), Palenque (7th century), El Tajín (10th century), and Chichén Itzá (11th century), as well as the Aztec pyramid of Tenayuca (13th century).

[71] The Pyramid of the Sun in the ruined city of Teotihuacán, built in the 3rd century AD, is the largest pyramid of the Mesoamerican cultures. In the foreground is another smaller pyramid with entrance stairways and places for sacrifice on the topmost plateau.

The ancient American pyramids rose in the midst of broadly laid out settlements, usually at the center of the community. Often they were directly surrounded by large plazas. Such temple courtyards can be found in Tihuanaco, a metropolis spread over almost 40 acres in the Andean highlands of Peru and dating from ca. 900 (72), or in the famous ball fields, such as that of Yagul (11th and 12th centuries). The latter were precisely laid out sunken rectangles surrounded by tribune-like earthen ramparts. These areas

[72] The temple courtyard of the city of Tihuanaco in Bolivia. Characteristic of such grounds are the relief pillars in the center of the courtyard.

were the site of the frequent ball games, often depicted in works of art, that were not only a form of sport, but also a ritualistic and symbolic ceremony whose significance is still not fully understood.

Especially in comparison with the primitive settlements of the European Middle Ages, the urban structures of the large Mesoamerican cities were highly sophisticated. As though drawn with a ruler, the streets intersected at right angles, the temples and public squares stood in precise alignment, and the residential areas were lined up neatly along broad

[73] Aerial view of the city of Chan Chan, located at the mouth of the Rio Mocho in Bolivia. Strong, easily defensible clay walls surround an exact, almost mathematically structured area of more than 7.8 square miles. The capital of the Chimú Empire, the city was conquered and plundered by the Incas in the 15th century.

[74] Map of the Aztec metropolis Tenochtitlán, drawn by the Spanish conquistador Hernando Cortes. The city, with navigable canals and a pyramid-temple in the center, stretched over more than 5.7 square miles. It was plundered and burned by Cortes's troops in 1521.

avenues (73, 74). In the Mayan culture, rectangular multiroomed apartment buildings predominated. Standing on low, multistepped earthen platforms, they were constructed of a light but weather-fast clay. Almost all the cities were populated with considerably more than 10,000 inhabitants, and the Aztec metropolis of Tenochtitlán, which was conquered by Cortes and eternalized in a colored map (74), was almost a Central American Venice. Traversed by canals, in the 16th century the city boasted more than 250,000 inhabitants. In contrast to the physical details of the cities, little is known about the social and economic life that took place in them. It is certain that these cities were the political and religious centers of the various tribes and served as administrative seats; possibly they also housed the central warehouses for food and raw materials, and were thus the production workshops for equipment and weapons of all kinds. In this sense, the Mesoamerican metropolises may well be comparable to the palace-cities of the Minoans on Crete (see page 14)—cultural centers, but at the same time very different from our modern conception of a city.

Machu Picchu: City on the airy heights

The discovery of the ruined city of Machu Picchu was one of the greatest archaeological sensations of the early 20th century (75, 76). In 1911 the American adventurer Hiram Bingham (the inspiration for the Hollywood adventurer Indiana Jones) was in fact searching for the Incan city of Vilcabamba. After a three-days' march from the ancient Inca capital of Cuzco, clambering up a steep slope to the top of a plateau, he unexpectedly came upon the completely overgrown ruins of a city above the valley of the Rio Urumbata on the eastern slopes of the Peruvian Andes—namely, Machu Picchu. An article coauthored by Bingham for the respected *National Geographic* magazine announced the city to the world in April 1913. Since that time, Machu Picchu in its breathtaking location has been the goal of an almost unending stream of tourists.

The location of the city even today remains a riddle in many respects, leading to a wide variety of speculations. The city belonged to the short-lived Incan empire that ruled the Andean region from approximately 1200 until the Spanish

[75] Machu Picchu: Inca ruins on a mountaintop surrounded by a grandiose Andean panorama.

conquest in the 16th century. The settlement was presumably abandoned in the course of Spanish expansion, but unlike so many other sites, it was not discovered and plundered by the Europeans. As a result, the buildings have remained in very good condition, with many still standing intact up to the roof line (76). The city has offered little by way of archaeological findings, however, because the inhabitants apparently took almost everything portable along with them as they fled from the *Conquistadors*.

[76] Machu Picchu: dwelling house. Built of carefully fitted field stones, the house is missing only the wooden elements of the gable roof. The numerous window openings are bridged with long architraves.

The character of the settlement still remains unclear. Every "real" Inca settlement is characterized by large warehouse buildings: The storage of a considerable supply of processed and gathered foodstuff was a pressing necessity for survival in this agriculturally inhospitable region. Such warehouses, however, are absent from Machu Picchu. At the same time, it is indisputable that people actually lived here on a permanent basis. In fact, the entire plateau, where it is not built up, is terraced and modeled into agricultural fields.

The settlement itself seems to be divided into two sections, a dwelling area and a temple area, connected by an entire system of streets and paths. The effect of the dwellings with their artfully arranged windows and gabled roofs is almost like that of row houses, exactly aligned and built parallel to each other. What appears from the distance to be a rather carelessly built rubble wall on closer inspection proves to be an engineering masterwork. Precisely cut stones were set on top of each other without mortar or other binding—a construction technique reminiscent of the pillars and stone buildings of ancient Greece (see page 18). But in Machu Picchu the method remains particularly mysterious because absolutely no knowledge of the tools and techniques that were used has survived. The only certainty is that the building materials were taken from a nearby quarry and carried with much effort up to the mountain plateau. Holes were bored into the hard rock in the quarry, and with the help of wet wooden pegs driven into the holes, the rock was cut along exact lines.

Probably constructed around 1450, Machu Picchu survived scarcely one hundred years. Most likely the settlement was not a city in the conventional sense, but rather a kind of villa or country palace of the Incan ruler (possibly Pachacutec). The few permanent residents of the city were presumably court servants who carried out the farm work and operated the various workshops, including a weaving shop. The unusual forms and interior furnishings and design of the "temples" (so designated because no more reasonable explanation for these buildings has been found), various theories about the astrological observations once practiced here, as well as the city's fascinating location have bequeathed Machu Picchu the aura of a mysterious and mystical Inca site.

Wooden huts and pueblos: Indian architecture of North America

North American Indian architecture is closely related to the social and especially the economic situation of the tribe in question. Especially in the northern reaches of the continent, the nomadic life predominated into the 19th century. An inevitable corollary of an economy based on hunting and gathering was the renunciation of permanent settlements. Instead, tent constructions dominated in summer, and ephemeral structures derived directly from nature in winter camps.

The sedentary tribes of the northern regions of the continent and of the prairie lived in small villages made up of community dwellings of different sizes. Such houses, which were up to 330 feet long, were inhabited by several family groups. The wooden buildings as a rule consisted of a quadrant of stable vertical posts to which the wall

[77] The front entrance of a wooden longhouse decorated with carvings: the Kwakiutl Indians on the coast of the American Northwest (Seattle/Vancouver). Reconstruction drawing.

boards were fastened. The posts also carried the weight of the roof, at times made of extremely heavy solid planks. The building technique is remarkable: Nails and dowels were unknown, and the individual pieces were bound together solely by means of mortises, notches, or ropes. The buildings were usually richly decorated with carving on the entrance side (77), but had no windows. At most, a closeable smoke-hole at the back of the building near the open hearth provided illumination. The floor was totally decked with wooden boards, and the interior was divided into compartments for the families who lived there.

[78] A multistory pueblo accessible by means of ladders: the Zuni Indians of New Mexico. Historical photo from 1879.

Many Indian tribes of the southern region (Arizona, New Mexico) lived, at least through the winter, in clay brick buildings, which could take on very divergent forms. Villages made up of small, separately built, box-like clay-brick houses predominated among the Papagos in southern Arizona. The Pueblo Indians of New Mexico developed another form, a multi-storied and labyrinthine conglomerate of block (or occasionally round) units, attached to each other—precisely the buildings designated as "pueblos" by the Spanish Franciscan priest Fray Morcos in 1539. Not only clay bricks were in use in these cultures. Some tribes, such as the Hopi Indians, also built layered stone structures which were then carefully plastered over.

The pueblo dwelling is a "one-house village" consisting of up to 800 connected room units. Built pyramid-fashion on top of one another, the rooms were normally accessible by ladder and could be entered by openings in the roof. The individual room units were connected throughout horizontally, but never vertically; exterior ladders were used to climb to another story. In this way, up to five stories could be placed on top of one another (78), and evidence of pueblos with more than 6,000 inhabitants has been found. The flat ceilings were constructed of solid wood coated with clay and plaster. On the lower stories the walls were nearly five feet thick, a massiveness that rapidly diminished with the increasing height of the building for reasons of weight. The top story of a pueblo was lightly constructed of clay and wattle instead of bricks.

The pyramid-shaped pueblos, mostly set on an even terrain, were ideally suited to defend against attacks. The solid walls of the bottom story were usually higher than the others, making the structure completely closed and inaccessible from the outside. Evidence of the compound building design of the pueblos reaches back to prehistoric time into the late phase of the Anasazi culture (Pueblo I Phase, after AD 700). Individual pueblos have undergone a building process that has lasted for centuries, and are still inhabited today. The structures were enlarged, altered, or modernized according to need. Aside from living quarters, the pueblo also included at least one central chamber or place which served as a community area for rituals and tribal meetings.

One variation of the pueblo adapted to the natural protective features of the landscape is the so-called cliff-dwelling, also an architectural conglomerate of rooms connected with each other. Because of their strategic locations on steep heights or within the protection of a remote mountain landscapes, such pueblos did without the defensively inaccessible ground story of the "flatland pueblos" and were therefore more irregular, variable, and "open" in design (79).

[79] The cliff pueblo of Mesa Verde, Colorado, situated high above the canyon, is built of a carefully prepared mixture of clay bricks and quarry stone.

Romanesque church architecture

The term "Romanesque" is derived from French and, as it implies, designates one of the cultural phenomena that followed the classical Roman era. In architectural history, it signifies the epoch of medieval architecture that parallels the consolidation of Western Latin culture as it increasingly demarcated itself from the other successors to ancient Rome, namely, Byzantine culture and Islam. The Romanesque center of gravity is, logically enough, in Italy and those lands north of the Alps that were blossoming just as the Romanesque style made its appearance. Chronologically, the Roman-esque period extended from the Carolingian to the Holy Roman epochs, (the 8th and 12th centuries AD), and can be further subdivided architecturally into an early Romanesque period (ending about 1000) and a golden age (11th and 12th centuries).

The primary impulse for Romanesque art and archi-tecture came from the church. In fact, building and painting were so fully integrated into the work of the church that few names of individual artists or archi-tects have survived, in stark contrast to the Renaissance era. For the medievals, results rather than the means of achieving them were foremost. Understandably, Ro-manesque architecture manifested itself chiefly in the

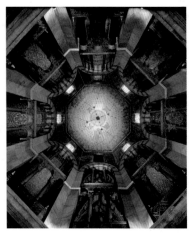

[80] The octagon of the palace chapel of Aachen Cathedral. The lower story serves as a church, while the upper was re-served for the imperial retinue as a formal room of state. In an excep-tion to the usual Romanesque anonymity, tradi-tion records Odo of Metz as the architect.

building of churches and cloisters. Buildings meant to display secular power were of secondary importance— and were in any case also largely interwoven with church concerns.

An early example of the connection of secular and ecclesiastical power is the Palatinate Chapel of the Aachen Cathedral (80). Built around 800 in the capital of the Carolingian empire, its octagonal ground plan clearly derived from the San Vitale church in Ravenna, built in the 6th century. The building was originally the throne room, i.e., an imposing secular structure in the palace of Charlemagne, and later became the heart of the Aachen Cathedral, which was constructed around it. The multistory interior, with a dome and round arches set on columns, clearly displays the striking leit-motifs of Romanesque architecture, which strove for maximum clarity of design in its major elements and borrowed a great deal from late classical architecture.

Just how much the basic forms of Romanesque architecture resemble those of the early Christian period can be seen in the ground plan of St. Michael's Basilica in Hildesheim, Germany, dating from the early 11th century (81). Unlike the cathedrals in Aachen or in Worms, it is not a central-plan building, but has the form of the basilica (see page 38), which was at that time increasingly built with a transept in front of the choir. This became the basic form of the late medieval church. The high point of German Romanesque architecture is the buildings of the Salian and Staufer dynasties, whose hegemony reached from northern France through Germany and Italy in the 11th and 12th centuries. Specifically, the cathedral at Speyer, Germany (built 1024–1106), boasts a filigree triple wall construction that points to the coming Gothic age.

The term "Norman Romanesque" designates the style as it developed under French influence, not only in France itself (St. Etienne in Caen), but throughout the area under Norman influence, extending from Italy to England, which had been conquered in the Battle of Hastings in 1066. Characteristics of Norman Roman-

1272–1307
England's Edward I establishes central administration there, grants Parliament of nobles taxation rights

1212–1250
Frederick II of Hohenstaufen, apex of the Holy Roman empire of the German nations

1226
Founding of the Teutonic Order, particularly influential in northeastern Europe (Marienburg, Poland)

1291
After 7 crusades, Christians abandon Acre, the last bulwark in Palestine

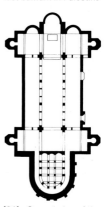

[81] Ground plan of the Basilica of St. Michael in Hildesheim, founded by Bishop Bernward in 1010.

esque include the organization of wall surfaces, an emphasis on pure ornamentalism, and development of the groin vault, in which two barrel vaults intersect at right angles—all developments that foreshadow the Gothic. Outside of France, prominent examples of Norman Romanesque include the cathedral of Durham (1091–1130) in England, whose exterior boasts almost Gothic flourishes; the cathedral and monastery at Monreale; and the massive and extravagantly ornamented cathedral of Cefalú (12th century in Sicily; 82). Another important witness to the French Romanesque is the monastery at Cluny, center of the Benedictine order of monks, begun in 1088.

In southern Italy, the Romanesque style was a highly eclectic, almost multicultural phenomenon. Non-Italian impulses derived largely from the Normans in Sicily and the Campania, and from the German Staufer dynasty under Frederick Barbarossa in Apulia (seen in the cathedrals of Bari, Trani, Bitonto, and Otranto). In northern Italy, however, an independent and strikingly new architectural conception began to develop in the 11th century, one which would later influence Renaissance architecture. An example of this style is the Campo dei Miracoli, a monumental ensemble constructed in the 11th century on the outskirts of Pisa (83). One characteristic of Italian ecclesiastical

[82] The Norman cathedral of Cefalú in Sicily.

buildings is the complete separation between a church and its bell tower (*campanile*), which stands to the side. The massive body of the cathedral in Pisa, a basilica with transept and dome above the center, appears almost Renaissance in style by virtue of its

[83] The Campo dei Miracoli in Pisa. The construction of the complex, consisting of baptistery, church, and campanile (the so-called "Leaning Tower of Pisa") was begun in 1063 and took two centuries to complete.

multi-story facade decorated with arcades and the applied ornamentation on the exterior of the lateral wings. Other Romanesque churches in northern and central Italian cities reveal equally impressive ornamentation, less in the form of relief than through the intentional use of variously colored building materials (the cathedral in Orvieto). Scrutiny of such examples of 12th- and 13th-century northern Italian architecture reveals how the Romanesque can flow into the Renaissance without a Gothic interlude.

The medieval fortress

One of the striking architectural images of the medieval period, in both the Byzantine East (see page 46) and the Latin West, is the fortress. Normally situated on inaccessible heights and thus visible at great distances, these massive examples of defensive architecture varied greatly in size, form, and appointment.

The fortress, so typical of the medieval period, is intrinsically linked with central aspects of contemporary feudal society. A finely organized system of aristocratic rule, ranging from small seats of local jurisdiction to regionally omnipotent courts (which were powerless in neighboring regions) was administered by a system of vassalage ranging from virtually powerless feudal lords up to the prince, king, or emperor. This feudal arrangement had developed into a network of dependencies whose core figure was the knight, an armed and mounted warrior with sufficient wealth to fulfill his military obligations. The basis of a knight's power lay in his ownership of land whose wealth could be exploited and in lordship over the vassals and serfs who tended the soil.

The heart of the fortress was the knight's residence, its elaborateness serving as a precise indication of his social and economic rank as a small *vavasour* or a regional lord. By around 1000, the knightly class had become so firmly established that it became common for a knight to increase his wealth—always with the permission of higher secular and ecclesiastical powers—by means of forays against irksome neighbors. As a result, at the turn of the 1st millennium, the need for protection increased and led to an emphasis on the defensive character of the fortress. The earliest fortresses were little more than inhabitable towers set on artificial heights and surrounded by palisades. (The so-called "Norman keep," which rises mightily on its solid, steep-sided pedestal even in the midst of a flat landscape, is a technically improved version of this early type of fortress). Knights began seeking sites on hills and mountain peaks, if at all possible, whose inaccessible height offered natural protection. The obvious disadvantage was that construction of a fortress in such a location could become a technically highly complicated undertaking. In flat landscapes, the fortresses began to acquire moats, earthen walls, and circular stone walls.

[84] Château Gaillard on the Seine, the royal fortress of Richard the Lionhearted, build ca. 1200. Ground plan showing elements typical of a fortress complex.

A typical medieval fortress (84) had three components. The military installation included walls, drawbridges, towers, possibly a preliminary fortification built up into a bastion, and storage areas for weapons. There was also a household area with workshops, store rooms, stalls, and cisterns or a spring. Finally, by the late 12th century, the originally very modest living quarters had developed into an imposing living area. The old keep, or *donjon*, became an inhabitable tower; the heart of the fortress had become a kind of domestic palace with a great

[85] "Eagle's nest" fortress Hocheppan in South Tirol, built around 1130.

hearth room, various smaller heated chambers, and at the center, the knights' hall and chapel. Sizes varied widely, from small rocky perches (85) to opulent and imposing castles (Wartburg), the immense monastic fortresses of the German Order in the eastern Ottoman empire (Marienburg, today in Poland), and the crusaders' fortresses in the eastern Mediterranean (Rhodes).

The placement of fortresses had a great impact on European settlement. They protected both borders and trade routes. Often, settlements began under fortress walls and later grew into cities (86). Some 30,000 fortresses are known throughout Europe, but the majority were abandoned and fell into ruins around 1500 when the invention of gunpowder necessitated new forms of fortification. Some, however, were transformed into imposing stately palaces and princely residences. Under the influence of 19th century historicism, the medieval fortress was stripped of its defensive or social functions and romanticized, and such sites became favored for aristocratic country estates, particularly in England and Scotland. Especially along the Rhine, a number

[86] Wine fields in the shadow of the fortress. The city of Kintzheim in Alsace owed its existence to the fortress, founded in 1190. At the beginning of the 16th century, the city obtained the ownership of the Staufer border-fortress to use as a refuge in times of war.

Art historian Georg Dehio concisely described the importance of brick to late medieval architecture of northern and eastern Germany: "North German architecture was built exclusively of brick. And from this given, architecture drew the full consequences. It did not accept brick as merely a technical help, but greeted it with imagination, adapted architectural forms to it, and in the process created a unified and truly brick style" (*History of German Art*).

The huge Gothic cathedrals in cities like Cologne and Paris are built of easily shaped, relatively light sandstone (whose susceptibility to environmental influences now poses immense restoration problems). The Baltic region, however, is virtually void of sandstone; the traditional building material here was baked clay bricks. The small-format building blocks can be formed at

[87]   Brick Gothic: Ornamentation on the portal of Mary's Church in Anklam, 13th century.

will, and all the stylistic elements of Gothic architecture proved imitable in brick: high, narrow frameworks, pointed and groin arches, and relieved portals and supports (87).

The socio-economic conditions that led to the emergence of the brick Gothic style stem from the rise of the Hanseatic League. This merchants' union of northern Germanic cities was primarily oriented toward Baltic trade and, as partially autonomous units, the Hanseatic cities were very prosperous in the 13th to 14th centuries. The wealth was enjoyed not only by city officials, but flowed into the hands of the citizen-merchants and clergy as well. Northern German brick Gothic expresses the desire of these groups for worthy and imposing architectural forms. From initially modest beginnings in the 12th century (the cathedrals of Ratzeburg, Schwerin, and Lübeck, all of which were founded by Henry the Lion), a magnificent brick architecture developed a century later, including cathedrals that hardly stand second to those of France and central Germany (88). Except in its more westerly reaches, the Hanseatic cities demonstrated their wealth by building not a single spectacular edifice per city, but an entire series of cathedrals. Even in a relatively small city like Lüneburg, made wealthy through salt mining, no fewer than four immense brick churches were built in the 15th century.

Northern German brick Gothic was not limited to sacred buildings; it was in fact not even especially devoted to them. Brick Gothic was the style of the day, and secular buildings with striking stepped gables can be found throughout the region in all architecture that aspired to particular dignity—private homes, communal buildings such as city halls, endowed complexes such as monasteries, impressively designed city gates (89), and offices and counting houses. These brick structures graced the leading Baltic cities of the late Middle Ages with a distinguished architecture, in large part still standing today.

Brick was the building material of choice in other regions where stone is rare. Many Italian cities built palaces and churches of brick in the

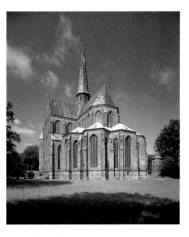

[88] Brick Gothic: The main church of the Cistercian monastery at Bad Doberan, after 1255.

13th and 14th centuries, and the sandstone facades of the cathedrals in Bologna, Ferrara, or Modena merely cover the brown bricks that are often still visible in the interior.

[89] Brick Gothic: The Holstein Gate in Lübeck, 15th century.

of fortresses now offer hotel accommodations for well-heeled tourists or serve as youth hostels.

Aspiring heavenward: The Gothic cathedral

It now seems ironic that "Gothic" as applied to architecture was initially a term of opprobrium. Intending to discredit a supposedly degenerate architectural style, the Italian architect and painter Giorgio Vasari (1511–1574), a fiery adherent of Italian Renaissance rationalism, used the term (derived from the barbarian Goths) to describe the "errors" typically found in large church and state buildings north of the Alps starting around 1300. Today the Gothic style is much admired as a bold and constructive style of religious architecture, widely prevalent in the 14th and 15th centuries in France, England, Germany, the Netherlands, and elsewhere.

Even more than the Romanesque cathedrals, the Gothic cathedrals had symbolic meaning: These gigantic structures aimed at the heavens are monuments of a society organized into guilds and classes, and dominated by the church into the last details of private life. Unlike Romanesque churches, which in spite of their considerable size were brought close enough to completion to be consecrated and used for religious services, Gothic cathedrals were often gigantic projects whose completion could not even be predicted. Depending on funding, the traditional builders' workshops remained more or less active for generations, and many Gothic cathedrals, such as that in Cologne, were not completed until hundreds of years after construction began. Typically, the eastern side of the cathedral with choir and transept was built first; the western components as a rule represent a later stage in construction.

[90] The Gothic cathedral. Cross-sectional view of the cathedral at Amiens (built ca. 1220).

No sharp break is evident between the Romanesque and Gothic styles. The cathedral of Durham (see page 71) may be interpreted as a transitional building. Strikingly Gothic elements, such as high, narrow individual elements or a typically Gothic organization of walls and space (90) are present in late Romanesque architecture; Gothic is marked by growing boldness in technical engineering. The increasing height of buildings and simultaneous minimizing of supports, and the bridging of space by means of filigree masonry arches, were not based on static calculations, but on trial and error. Thus, the collapse of a just-completed structure (such as the cathedral of Beauvais in 1284), or a pause for the sake of necessary repairs, was common.

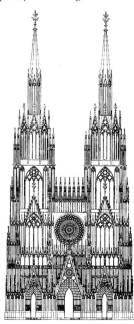

[91] The western front of the minster in Strasbourg. The outline, measuring more than 9 feet high, is the prototype of design drawings that were preserved and widely shared by the workshops of the building guilds. Building plans for continuation of the work (see page 85).

Over time, the ever-decreasing mass of the architectural skeleton became bolder, the walls ever lighter due to large windows, and the jagged pointed ornamentation on the immense exteriors became ever more bizarre.

Despite these developments, architectural planning remained mainly limited to large-scale views of the project. Technical data in the modern sense were lacking, but design requirements were handed down in the builders' guilds and workshops through the generations (91). Size itself was a characteristic attribute of the Gothic: The cathedral of Amiens (from 1220) offered space for the city's entire population. The cathedral was not only the center of the city, but could also be seen from great distances and dominated the sur-

[92] Monastery church of St. Denis, Paris. The choir passage inside the church is a pioneer work of early Gothic.

rounding area. The towers grew to immense heights, proportional to cathedrals' vast structural volume, and often remained unfinished for years. The tower of the minster at Strasbourg, France, was completed in 1439, and at 425 feet resembled a 40-story skyscraper; those of the minsters in Ulm and Freiburg (Germany), as well as that of the Cathedral of St. Stephen in Vienna, are almost as high.

The center of early Gothic development was the Île-de-France region around Paris. The pioneering work began in 1135 when the church of the monastery of St. Denis (founded in the 7th century) was renovated with a circular passage around the choir (92). The high Gothic style is also marked by French influence, as represented in the famous cathedrals of Chartres, Reims, and Amiens. By the 14th century, the late Gothic took on various national and regional characteristics, seen for example in Prague (in the work of the Parler family stone masons) and in the flamboyant style of the Netherlands. In England, the Gothic style carried political implications. In the 13th century, in light of growing English-French rivalry, Gothic became a national style intended to suppress the trauma of the Norman-

Romanic invasion and provide an opportunity for the nobility to establish a shared identity.

Gothic style is largely, but not exclusively, limited to ecclesiastical architecture. In the late Middle Ages, wealthy cities often adopted this style for their impressive public buildings. Prominent examples can be seen foremost in the cities of Flanders with their unique, self-confident architectural melding of Gothic and Renaissance design (City Hall, Bruges; Cloth Hall, Ypres), as well as in Eastern Europe, in Thorn and Wrocaw (today's Poland), for example. The Gothic also played a modest role in the building of castles and forts (see page 73). As a late medieval style, Gothic was evident in central and northern Europe, even into the 17th century (for example, the Jesuit Church of Cologne). The so-called "Gothic revival," centered in England around 1800, demonstrated both the broad acceptance granted to the originally negative term and encouraged architectural historicism in general (see page 122). In the United States, the brick Gothic style was often adopted for public buildings, particularly museums (the original Smithsonian building) and university buildings.

[93] The cathedral of Wells, England, was begun in 1089 in the Romanesque tradition, but remodeled in the Gothic style after 1340. Typical of English Gothic, the striking tower, constructed on an almost perfectly square ground plan, stems from the 15th century.

The Monastery Plan of St. Gallen:

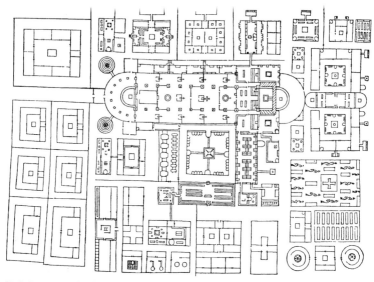

[94] The plan of St. Gallen displays an ideal ground plan of a Benedictine monastery of the Carolingian age. The church, cloister, and monks' cells stand in the center, with the utility and domestic areas grouped around them.

The building plan of the monastery at St. Gallen, Switzerland, is a unique—and inestimable—aid to understanding early medieval architecture (94). Drawn on a piece of calfskin parchment about 43 x 31 inches, the plan depicts a Carolingian monastery complex dating from ca. 820. In precise detail, the drawing indicates all that belonged to a monastery of that age, with particular attention paid to the carefully defined distinctions among the buildings and the tracts of land that formed the economic and agricultural basis of the monastic community. The St. Gallen plan is the only such scale drawing that reproduces the layout and structures of an architectural complex between

the decline of the classical world and the 12th century.

The "blueprint" also shows in exemplary fashion how much the contemporary understanding of building plans differed from a modern one. The St. Gallen plan did not serve as an aid in the process of building, but rather served to provide an ideal model; an outline for a monastery whose main tasks were prayer and work—*ora and labora*, the rule of the Benedictine order—founded in 529.

Various building plans had been drawn already in prehistoric times and in the advanced cultures of the ancient world, beginning with the Sumerians of Mesopotamia. These, too, emphasized the ground plan, the exact lines of which were etched as if with a ruler into a tablet, usually of clay. Such "plans" probably served as orientation aids in the building process. The subjects of such drawings included not only sacred and burial complexes, but also simple houses. The ancient Egyptians expanded the repertoire of architectural drawings to include a profile and detailed view, leading to an accumulation of architectural know-how which was partially forgotten in the classical Greek and Roman cultures. Drawing plans for buildings are in fact wholly unknown in the archaic and classic periods; instead, building intentions were conveyed in the form of written language seen in surviving, often highly complex, verbal references to design, size, and construction. Actual architectural plans first occur again in Hellenistic-Roman times, usually as outlines of architectural details. Such drawings were rarely transferred to an external medium, but appear in the form of extremely fine line drawings—often badly eroded and hardly legible—scratched onto the walls or floors of the buildings themselves. This practice was still common in the construction of medieval churches.

Beginning with the late Gothic period of the 12th century, building plans became the order of the day in Western architecture. As in the case of the large outline of the front of the minster at Strasbourg, or a similar outline for the front of the cathedral at Cologne, they primarily served to communicate precise ideas of design among the guild workshops that were involved with a project over the long term.

In the evaluation of architectural plans, a distinction is necessary between the various functional uses they served. The purpose of a given plan determines the level of exactitude and degree of precision with which a drawing is made. Rough architectural sketches and visionary architectural pictures aid in general theoretical reflection or in the decision-making process on important characteristics of the building. In contrast, splendidly detailed plans and outlines are traditionally an element in advanced discussions between the architects and the person(s) having something constructed. In order for the architect to secure the contract, the prospective "customers" need to see the representative character of their building before their very eyes. Finally, the actual plans of the architects (ground and floor plans, cross-sectional views, outlines, profiles) are of a rather sober technical sort with many measurements that serve a number of functions. They act as the plans and legal documents for carrying out the construction, drawing up the bill, and sometimes for legal disputes. In contrast to the other categories of drawing, exact scale is essential on these "blueprints."

Alberti and Palladio: Protagonists of Renaissance architecture

The Italian term *rinascitá*, from which our modern word "renaissance" derives, was used as early as the 14th and 15th centuries to describe the awakening interest in the fine arts and architecture with the revival of the classical Roman world. This new artistic and architectural movement, which became increasingly dominant in the secular domain, stood in sharp contrast to the clerical stamp of the Romanesque Middle Ages. Unlike the artistic anonymity that was typical of the Romanesque period, the Renaissance brought forth great numbers of prominent artists and architects—a phenomenon whose roots lay in the enormous changes in the social, intellectual, and economic framework introduced by humanism. For the first time in history, the concept of artistic or architectural geniuses who followed their own imagination arose. They were motivated by unique creative impulses, and not exclusively by the tasks set by the patron who awarded the contract.

Closely connected with the political and economic flowering of the city states (Venice, Florence, Rome, and others), the phenomenon of the Renaissance was initially limited to the Italian peninsula. Only later did the Renaissance cross the Alps into northern Europe, largely through a growing acquaintance of northern artists with the works of individual outstanding Renaissance architects, such as Andrea Palladio. The entirely different historical and political frameworks of the two regions, however, meant that the developments in northern Europe never truly mirrored those of the Italian Renaissance. The beginnings of the Renaissance in Italy ran roughly parallel to the Gothic developments in Germany and France; in a sense, the Italian Renaissance obviated a Gothic development, whose few traces occur in Italy only as details, seen in flying buttresses and arched windows that were incorporated into Renaissance buildings. The term "Renaissance" generally refers to the art of the more than a century and a half between 1350 and 1520, which can be broken into an early Renaissance period (late 13th and early 14th centuries, typified by the Palazzo Pubblico in Siena), the high Renaissance, and culminating in the late Renaissance or mannerist period, which in turn led to the Baroque movement of the second half of the 16th century.

The leitmotif of the Renaissance is its rediscovery of the classical world in painting, sculpture, and architecture. In this sense, however, the classic age refers only to ancient Rome, and not to Greece. In many Italian cities the ruins of Roman monuments were still on view for admiration. In contrast, from the time of the Ottoman conquest of the southern Balkan peninsula, Greek antiquity was sealed off as if behind an iron curtain, and existed in the West only as a literary ideal for philosophers and scientists (see page 116). The event that ignited the spark of a new architecture that would turn over Romanesque principles was the rediscovery of the *Ten Books on Architecture*, written by the Roman author Vitruvius around the time of Christ, but subsequently lost. An early medieval copy of the books was found in the library of the monastery at St. Gallen. Copies of the copy—and soon translations—were very quickly and widely disseminated. Especially interesting was Vitruvius's discussion of the order of columns (Ionic, Doric, Corinthian), which immediately led to an intensive architectural activity based on these ancient designs. These were all the more easy to understand because of the many classic examples still extant.

The first protagonist in this drama was the all-around Renaissance genius Leon Battista Alberti (1404–1472), who was not only an architect, but also a poet, musician, natural scientist, and—in his youth—a respected sportsman. The financially independent aristocrat took an interest in the

1515–1547
Francis I king of France
1517
Luther posts 95 theses in Wittenberg
1529
Turks at the gates of Vienna for the first time
1530
Melanchthon composes Protestant confession for Diet of Augsburg, which is rejected by Habsburg emperor Charles V
1555
Peace of Augsburg grants confessional freedom to German princedoms
1572
10,000 French Huguenots die in St. Bartholomew's Day massacre
after 1589
Henry IV of Bourbon settles religious conflict in France
1598
Edict of Nantes grants freedom of conscience in France

[95]   Leon Battista Alberti. Profile on a bronze medallion by Pisanello.

[96]   Classic order of columns, placed on top of one another according to Vitruvius. The pilaster style, starting at the ground level, is Doric, Ionic, and Corinthian. Facade of the Palazzo Rucellai, Florence, 1446–1451, built from plans by Leon Battista Alberti.

[97]   Andrea Palladio. Portrait.

principles of architectural theory (see page 98/99), studied Vitruvius intensively, and toward the end of his life authored his own book on architecture. Closely modeled on its Roman predecesor, *De Re Aedificatoria* (*On Architecture*; first edition published posthumously in 1485) was also written in ten volumes, in a Latin similar to that of Vitruvius. Alberti remained a theoretician, but his work had immense influence on successive generations of architects. Although few designs of his were actually built, they all served as prime examples of Renaissance architecture. In addition to the use of the ancient Roman triumphal arch as an entrance for churches (for example, San Andrea, Mantua), Alberti's main interest lay in the application of the classic orders of columns in facades (96).

In contrast to the theoretician Alberti, the architect Andrea Palladio (97), who lived roughly a century later (1508–1580), was primarily a practitioner. As a representative of the late Renaissance, Palladio in a sense combined and "ennobled" all that had been formulated by the generations of architects that preceded him, including Brunelleschi, Bramante, Michelangelo, Raphael, Sangallo, Filarete, and many others. More than one hundred of Palladio's designs are still standing today, and he made himself a name as innovator in many areas. The Palladian motif in window design, for example, designates an arcade of three rounded windows in which a central, higher window is flanked by two smaller openings (basilica in Vicenza). In addition to his numerous public buildings in northern Italian cities, Palladio's villas brought him renown; even centuries later they stand as ideal architectural images of the late Renaissance (98, 99).

Palladio also authored works on architecture and provided the first well-grounded description of the classical monuments of the city of Rome (*Le antichitá di Roma*, first edition 1554), which remained a standard work for more than 200 years. In 1556 he illustrated a broadly published Italian translation of Vitruvius, and finally, in 1570, published his own richly illustrated treatise, *Quattro libri dell'architettura* (*Four Books on Architecture*). Both as a practicing architect and as a theoretician, Palladio was a standard-bearer. Enthusiastic admirers such as Vincenzo Scamozzi and Inigo Jones enthusiastically carried forth his architectural ideals and established the phenomenon known as Palladianism, which spread throughout Europe and survived into the 19th century.

[98]   Garden facade of the Villa Cornaro, in Piombino Dese, Italy. Built in 1553 according to a design by Palladio.

[99]   Original design for the Villa Pisani in Montagnana. From Palladio's *Quattro libri dell'architettura*, published in 1570.

Palaces, churches, and villas: Models of Renaissance architecture

In principle, Renaissance architecture adheres to a clearly rational and transparent structure, consisting of a few clear geometrical forms. The

[100] An "ideal" city of the Renaissance: painting by Pietro della Francesca, ca. 1470. The rationally designed buildings rise above a terrain consisting of a mathematically exact grid. In the midst of the palazzo-like house stands a church modeled on the classical round temple. Ideal cities of this sort were occasionally realized to some extent, the most famous example being the star-shaped fortified city of Palmanova, near Udina in northern Italy, built according to plans by Vincenzo Scamozzi after 1593.

circle, square, and rectangle form the basis of the ground plan, while the sphere, hemisphere, cube, elongated cube, and cylinder provide the volume. The entirety of the design is also rationally proportioned, at times literally infused with theory (see page 98). Diverse attempts to produce an "ideal city" composed of a harmonious combination of all these elements, either on paper or in actual structures, make these basic forms and principles clear (100). In the Renaissance, these basic forms were combined with antique classical motifs. Columns, pilasters, capitals drawn from the various orders, triumphal-arch motifs and domed halls all constitute references to classic Roman architecture. The building-block form of construction predominated, often allied with a striking antique effect on the ground floor—that is, the blocks were not smoothed, but appear bossed and rough in order to impart a defensive-aggressive character to the building.

Three outstanding building types prevailed in Renaissance architecture. As a type of building, the palazzo (101) is the direct product of the political, economic, and social structure of the northern Italian city states after 1200. The palazzo served two basic functions: either as a generously proportioned public building (usually used as a city hall), or as a private residential building for an urban-aristocratic family. Many northern Italian cities are studded with these primarily three-story cubic structures, including the rusticated ground (or socket) level, the *piano nobile* above it used as the lordly private domain, and a low-ceilinged third level—a design which until today is an emblem of the local aristocracy. The palazzo as an architectural form experienced a revival in the Baroque period of the 17th and 18th centuries, occurring in Bourbon-ruled Naples, for example, as impressively large block buildings erected around courtyards and reached by complicated stairways. Such houses served individual nobles not only as residences, but also as capital investments, since they also contained numerous rented apartments.

During the Renaissance, ecclesiastical architecture received particular emphasis. In Italy, the prosperity of the cities was synonymous with the wealth of the clergy. Their almost limitless financial resources were the foundation for the construction of churches whose dimensions and construction times were literally unforeseeable. There was work enough for generations of architects, and often the direction of a building project was handed down from father to son. The hallmark of Renaissance churches is on the one hand their magnificent facades, designed down to the smallest detail, and on the other, the dome, a motif borrowed from classical Rome and found in its ideal form in the Pantheon (2nd century AD). It was precisely the dome that offered ground for innovation and experimentation, and thus became a guarantee for lasting architectural fame. Between 1418 and 1436, Filippo Brunelleschi's daring construction of a dome over the Florentine cathedral above an octagonal base became the standard for all other Renaissance architects. The definitive Renaissance dome was the round dome on St. Peter's in Rome, erected under Michelangelo's direction (102). Matching the Roman Pantheon in diameter, Michelangelo altered the cross-sectional profile by

[101] The Palazzo Medici in Florence was built between 1444 and 1464 by Michelozzo de Bartolommeo (1396–1472) and served as the prototype of the three-story city palace with a rusticated ground floor (sockel). Reconstructed drawing of the original building.

rejecting a true semi circular form. The height of the dome is exaggerated in comparison to the diameter of the base. Unlike the Pantheon, the dome not only forms a striking characteristic of the exterior of the building, but is also visible at a great distance. True to the Renaissance love of rationality, the full height above the floor corresponds to the diameter of the domed area. St. Peter's became a convention of Renaissance architecture which was often quoted later, as in the Baroque dome of St. Paul's Cathedral in London and in the Capitol in Washington, D.C.

[102] The dome of St. Peter's attained a height of 433 feet above floor level with a diameter of almost 138 feet. Begun in 1547, the construction was directed by Michelangelo Buonarroti (1475–1564), based on a variation of a design by Bramante.

The Renaissance adopted not only the external look of classical Rome, such as architectural and graphic forms, but also pursued its lifestyle. Classical literature had preserved many images of leisurely and relaxed aristocratic life as pursued in magnificent townhouses and villas outside the city gates (see page 31). These classical images were taken up by the wealthy as a direct model. Just as in the days of old, a comfortable country villa became the necessary counterweight to a city palazzo and provided an ultimate refuge from hectic urban life. The construction of such country estates with their sometimes exorbitant architectural luxury, artfully designed gardens, and "natural" ambiance provided an excellent task for Renaissance architects. Numerous such villas are to be found in the vicinity of almost all northern Italian cities, and the master of villa design was Andrea Palladio himself (see page 87). The villa

[103]   The Palladio bridge in Prior Park in Bath, England.

served as both a building and a lifestyle; rarely in history has the ancient world been so thoroughly adapted and raised to the standard of contemporary life as in the Italian Renaissance.

Individual approaches to the Renaissance: 16th-century English and French castles

Although the terms "Renaissance" and "Baroque" seem to imply that they are two fully separate stylistic epochs, a variety of factors lead modern art historians to deny that either period can be designated as a clearly defined age. Widespread in France and England during the 16th century, the Baroque tendency expressed itself—with a good deal of regional variation—in Renaissance-like forms and imposing architectural structures, manifested chiefly in palaces and elaborate country estates. As in the Renaissance, Baroque architecture was largely rooted in royalist-absolutist concepts; thus it is advisable both from the point of view of art history and from that of social history to see the architecture of these two "ages" as developments along a continuum.

The French Renaissance palaces in the environs of Paris and in the Loire valley, which was the favorite hunting preserve of the court, owe a certain debt to Renaissance influence as it manifested itself in northern Italy. Under the monarchs Francis I (reigned 1515–1547) and Henry II (reigned 1547–

1558), the French court drew inspiration for the possibilities of using architecture as a means of self-presentation, a symbolic medium for the display of power. However, the social context of the Renaissance in Italy was entirely different from that in France, where there were no republican city states with an urgent need to express their more-or-less pluralistic and internally competitive aristocratic societies. On the contrary, in France all development was a reflection of royal splendor. Almost all the

[104] The palace of Chambord. Front view. Built 1519–1559 in the Loire Valley between Tours and Orléans, the luxurious country palace is constructed around a fortified core.

palace construction of this period was either directly commissioned by the king or indirectly by court aristocrats (and even then usually in the ruler's name and for the glory of France, which was at the time involved in competition with Burgundy).

Few buildings, however, were as large and architecturally overdecorated as the palace of Chambord (104), which was begun in 1519 at the behest of Francis I. Châteaus and palaces tended to be rather small architectural preserves, not megalomaniac structures like the famous castles at Blois, Fontainebleau, or Chenonçeau. Provided with a maximum of splendid architectural decoration, the ground plans of most palaces were relatively small and simple. Usually square in form, the building enclosed a small inner court-yard, and included round towers with cone-shaped roofs at the corners. Rooms for domestic life, ceremonies of state, and household work were clearly distinguished from one another by the elaborateness of the architecture, and a beautifully designed decorative garden was integral to the concept. Historical arguments aside, French palace architecture of the 16th century, in its architectural and conceptual details, is primarily ascribed to the Renaissance. But at root, the phenomenon stems rather from the Gothic. The "type" of the French country palace with its decorative flourishes made its appearance as a national icon as early as the 14th and 15th centuries, when numerous illustrated texts already refer to this tradition (105).

In the same way, and just as questionably, the architecture of Elizabethan England is often defined as "Renaissance." In England, however, beyond the glory of a long and continuous rule (Elizabeth, reigned 1558–1603) and the economic prosperity that accompanied it, there seems to be nothing behind the architectural development but a very showy manifestation of a national architectural tradition. This development has little to do with the Italian Renaissance, in fact, and is rather a phenomenon of Gothic design, in this case in a typically Britannic form. At the core of the so-called "English Renaissance" lies the Tudor style, named after the ruling house, in particular King Henry VIII (reigned 1509–1547). Tudor architecture, however, is a distinctly ornamental style based on brick—England's answer to the general lack of

[105] The palace as French national symbol: The Gothic walls of Château Saumur on the Loire offer a fitting example. Illustration from the *Book of Hours of the Duc de Berry*, ca. 1480.

93

[106] Longleat House in the county of Wiltshire combines Tudor brick technology with Renaissance style. Begun in 1572.

sufficient wood. Furthermore, because the bricks themselves are small, brick buildings are well-suited to structural ornamentation. The palace at Hampton Court east of London, begun by Henry VIII in the 1530s, is the most famous example of Tudor architecture, demonstrating both the ornamental possibilities of brick building techniques as well as the Gothic origins of the style. In contrast, the epitome of the Elizabethan Renaissance is Longleat House, Wiltshire. The Renaissance-style palazzo (see page 87), built on an almost symmetrical ground plan, employed basically the same building techniques, but is designed as a perfectly proportioned three-story structure with a parapet at the roof level.

Renaissance influence: Palladianism in Europe and the United States

No other architect, past or present, can compare with Andrea Palladio in terms of his singular influence on later architectural history. He achieved immortality not only through his numerous buildings, but also through his widely-read writings, which carried his architectural ideas far beyond the borders of Italy. Already during his lifetime, and to an even greater extent after his death, Palladio became a kind of star of the architectural world, giving the impulse for what has become known as Palladianism in modern architectural history. The Englishman Inigo Jones (1573–1652) was an enthusiastic admirer of Palladio's ideas and spent several months studying the master's buildings in northern Italy as well as the classical ruins of Rome in 1613. Carrying what he learned back to England, he became the founder of the English Palladian style, seen particularly in two outstanding examples, the Queen's House in Greenwich (built 1629–1635) and the Banqueting House in Whitehall (built 1619–1622; 107), which established the Palladian norms that would be so often copied and varied. Jones remained true to Palladio throughout almost his entire career. His work, much respected in England, was studied and adapted by succeeding generations of English architects. Palladianism thus forms an important root of the English Baroque style, seen in the work of such prominent architects as Christopher Wren, Nicholas Hawksmoor, and John Vanbrugh during the 17th and 18th centuries.

[107] Inigo Jones: Banqueting House, Whitehall, London, built 1619–1622. The rusticated ground floor (sockel) with a two-story building and showy roof parapet rising above it are based on Palladian models.

It was not only in England that Palladio's work exerted a powerful influence. On the European continent, Elian Holl (1573–1646), the city architect of Augsburg, Germany, borrowed directly from Palladio in numerous buildings, his masterpiece being the still extant multi-storied Augsburg Rathaus with its magnificent facade (108). In the course of the 17th century, the Palladian influence spread throughout Europe, taking on various regional

[108] Elias Holl: The Augsburg Rathaus, reconstructed in the 1960s after its complete destruction in World War II.

differences, seen in villas, palaces, and public buildings in Poland, Prussian Sweden, Denmark, and Finland.

A second period of Palladian influence was initiated through the "rediscovery" of the structures erected by the Palladians of the 17th century— buildings that had long been forgotten amid the more extravagant splendor of the Baroque. This so-called "neo-Palladianism" can be understood as an early form of the later classicism (see page 114/15) that once again sought its inspiration in the building styles of ancient Rome. A phenomenon of the first half of the 18th century, this extremely important phase of architectural history preceded the rediscovery of classical ancient Greece. Once again, the initial impulses came from England; especially significant figures in neo-Palladianism include Lord Burlington (1684–1753) and Colen Campbell (1676–1728). Campbell became famous for his country houses and villas, which were inspired to an equal extent by the work of Palladio and by the Italian Renaissance. In addition, his richly illustrated treatise *Vitruvius Britannicus* (first edition published in 1715) came to serve as a textbook for contemporary architecture.

In the form of an ennobling architectural gesture, neo-Palladianism carried over into the early buildings of the English colonies of North America as they struggled for independence. This form of classicism had its roots in the desire of the colonists to lend a veneer of tradition and history to the revolutionary struggle. Understandably, American classicism borrowed from the English model to a small extent, and was also inspired by the architectural history of France, with its classicism that was motivated by both Renaissance and ancient Roman impulses.

In many ways comparable to Leon Battista Alberti, Thomas Jefferson was also a well-rounded "universal genius" directly following the Renaissance model. His architectural ideas derived not directly from Palladio, but more generally from his own quite comprehensive library collection. The buildings he designed (including the State Capitol in Richmond, Virginia, and both his estate Monticello and the University of Virginia in Charlottesville) achieve a complex interweaving of neo-Palladianism, French Renaissance, Baroque, and English early classicism into an American pseudo-traditional style (109), which represents the culmination of the Palladian influence.

[109] The Rotunda of the University of Virginia (built 1817–1826) in Charlottesville, Virginia was constructed according to plans by Thomas Jefferson in the Palladian style.

The Theory of Architecture: Building Philosophy in Action

A dictionary entry for architectural theory defines it as a striving to comprehend the normative laws that underlie architecture, in both its formal and its symbolic aspects, and the attempt to formulate these as ideal models. In the process, architectural theory draws from concrete historical building codes and purposes (for example, construction norms and proportions, or religious symbolism) on one hand, and from philosophical and aesthetic considerations on the other. In both cases, the goal of architectural theory is always to formulate and justify an ideal. The theory of architecture is found in written texts and in visual representations, both drawn or modeled, of architecture—but not in actual buildings. The boundary between real architecture and the basically analogous architectural imagination, however, is not absolute.

The beginnings of architectural theory lie in classical antiquity—at least the first evidences of written treatment of the subject stem from this era (even if specific details have generally not survived). These earliest authors are either concerned with their own building plans or attempt to come to terms critically with the works of another architect. Among the pioneers number Theodoros of Samos and the team of Chersiphron and Metagenes, who were involved in the construction of the large Ionic temples of Asia Minor in the 6th century BC (including the temple of Artemis at Ephesus and the temple of Hera on Samos). The earliest writings, in general, present and justify their own designs.

In contrast, the writings of the late classic and Hellenistic architects (Hippodamos, Hermogenes, Pytheos and others) with their fundamental reflections on ideal form (*symmetria*), already possess the character of general theorizing. Having survived the centuries intact, the epitome of ancient architectural theory is the encyclopedic work of the Roman architect Vitruvius, *Ten Books on Architecture*, composed around the time of Christ, in which the author demanded for the first time that architecture be ranked as an art.

Since the 12th century, Vitruvius's work has been the *vade mecum* of all architects; moreover, during the Renaissance, having been richly illustrated and translated into various languages, Vitruvius's books became the cornerstone of all attempts to systematize architecture and place it on a scientific basis. Following in the footsteps of Alberti (see page 84), soon every architect of serious pretensions produced at least one architectural tract, often dealing with the problems of the orders of columns and the analogies between architectural proportions and those of the human body. Such works—whether by Italians such as

The Theory of Architecture: Building Philosophy in Action

Serlio, Vignola, Filarete, and Scamozzi or by northern Europeans such as Ryff, Blum, or Ditterlin—tended to be richly illustrated.

Beyond these concerns with the formal and proportional maxims of classic architecture, practical considerations also became the focus of architectural theory. Forerunners of the so-called "pattern books" of basic architectural forms (which first appeared in the late 18th century and were increasingly circulated even within circles of amateur architects) offered "ideal ground plans" oriented on geometrical figures and described the "best" proportions for various formal details. In all cases, copies and variations of once-available drawings were typical: There was no copyright in the modern sense. These architecture books made the drawings of a Palladio or Serlio, whether as faithfully traced copies or as imaginative variations, available to the widest possible audience between the 16th and the early 19th centuries.

Totally inimical to such practical needs, however, was French architectural theory during the age of absolutism. Here for a time theorists pursued a "retarding" special course (which later resulted in important consequences). Delorme, Perrault, and Blundell are the standard bearers of the so-called academy approach, which was rooted on the one hand in the position of architecture as a recognized science within the *Academie Française*, and on the other hand in the attempt to connect the architectural norms of the Italian Renaissance with components of a national French architecture. The resulting buildings first and foremost dogmatically conformed to the functional needs of absolutism, as well as its need to impress. Architecture was a court art. These rigid standards also led to reflection upon appropriate architectural forms for less privileged social groups, and thus moved away from the theretofore unquestioned devotion of architecture to the classic standards of a Vitruvius. Around the middle of the 18th century, French architectural dogmatism transformed itself into an innovative intellectual approach based on a classicism drawn from ancient Greek traditions of form and functions (see page 114), exemplified by Laugier and others.

The critiques leveled by historicism and, later, Art Nouveau at the norms of the architectural past, in particular classical norms, set in motion an explosive broadening of architectural theory. Almost every new stream of architecture from the mid-19th century to the immediate present has been accompanied by a theoretical argument that legitimizes the tendency, provides a basis for it, and demarcates it from past theories or competitive schools.

The Victory of Ornamentation: King, Nobility, and Clergy:

King, nobility, and clergy: The historical context of the Baroque

"The Baroque speaks the same language as the Renaissance, but in a degenerated dialect. Its classic orders of columns, entablatures, pediments, etc. are altered with great arbitrariness and in the most various manners ... many architects compose their works in constant *fortissimo* .... In default of an organic surface, [the Baroque] required that what had been decoration during the Renaissance now express strength and passion, which were to be achieved through coarseness and simplification .... A direct result of this roughness was the desensitization of the eye .... The units of the building begin to move; in particular, the pediments begin ... to fall apart, to tumble and swing in all directions .... These are fevered dreams of architecture."

Such are the unflattering words with which Jacob Burckhardt, the famed Swiss historian of art and culture, described the Baroque style in his panegyric of 1855 (*Der Cicerone*). Burckhardt himself would later revise this negative judgment, but it nonethe-less bequeathed a standard of taste that until very recently was shared by many of those interested in art. Only recently has a more positive view emerged, partly in response to recent enthusiasm over Tiepolo.

The Baroque style that held sway in the late 16th to the mid-18th centuries is characterized by an expressive pathos and richness of ornamentation, by swirling lines and light-and-shadow effects, and by excessive decoration including gilded plaster ornaments, floating putti, and brilliant color. In today's understanding, Baroque denotes not merely a style of architecture, sculpture, and painting, but is a more general cultural phenomenon encom-passing music, theater, and fashion, as well as furniture design, book illustration, and literature. This universality, as well as the unusually eclectic formal canon of the style, was in fact something wholly new in the history of Western culture—

something that Jacob Burckhardt was one of the first to realize. One can argue about the Baroque aesthetic, its tendency to disguise, and its function as an imposing theatrical backdrop; but at the same time one must admit that the normative power of the ancient classical world as it had been definitively formulated by the Renaissance culture of the 15th and 16th centuries was almost radically overturned by Baroque ideology.

[110] Pioneer work in the Baroque: With its curving lines, the Il Gesù church in Rome, built by Giacomo da Vignola beginning in 1568, became the prototype of the Baroque facade.

The Baroque style was a direct outgrowth of absolutism; the two go hand in hand. Baroque is the symbolization of opulence, wealth, and the power of the upper classes. In this sense, its buildings and paintings are a reflection of the social structures of its age, in particular, the close interweaving of church and secular power. It is no accident that the main emphasis of the style falls on churches and monasteries (including their interiors), together with palaces, princely residences, courtly and pompous interior decoration, and secular buildings designed to impress the beholder. It was, after all, the court, the aristocracy, and the clergy who commissioned the work.

The Baroque is a reflection of absolutism in another sense as well. As a style, it was itself absolutist and authoritarian. In a unique manner, the Baroque concept of art and decoration insisted on its own preeminence and allowed no competition. In the process, the Baroque became the universal denominator: Hardly a church, no matter how old and honorable, remained untouched. Everything stemming from the past was subject to remodeling and was redesigned in the Baroque style. At the very least the interiors, and all too often the exteriors as well, were radically recreated in the "new style."

Curving gable façades and cornices disguised old and venerable facades; the narrow columns that separated the nave and side aisles in churches were rebuilt into massive, richly ornate pilasters (with the columns literally reconstructed in the process); barrel vaults and domes were integrated; profiled decorations of gilded marble plaster, relief columns, and floating angels were added; and walls were sheathed in colored stone paneling (111). Numerous Romanesque-Lombard buildings, Gothic, and even Renaissance structures were robbed of their character, indeed of their history, through these massive assaults.

[111] The Baroque as "equalizer": the originally Gothic church of Santa Maria del Carmine in Naples was remodeled in a Spanish Baroque style in 1755. Today, only an architectural expert can distinguish the few surviving Gothic elements—an example of the triumph of the Baroque.

Beginning in the late 16th century, the Baroque adopted very individualistic regional variations. The core of the movement lay in the mannerism of the late Italian Renaissance. In southern Italy, however, from the 17th century onward architecture primarily

[112] Austrian Baroque: the Benedictine monastery at Melk was built on a hill high above the Danube by Jakob Prandtauer between 1702 and 1746.

displayed elements of the cluttered and bulky Spanish style (seen in the cathedrals of Saragossa and Santiago de Compostella). North of the Alps, particularly in southern Germany (i.e., the princely residence in Würzburg, the Wieskirche in Steingaden) and Austria (112), an airy light-flooded Baroque and Rococo architecture came into being. In France, as in England, the Baroque assumed yet another form in which the formal canon adhered to Renaissance tradition (113).

[113] English Baroque: St. Paul's Cathedral, London, constructed between 1675 and 1710 by Sir Christopher Wren.

The triumph of appearance over reality: Methods of design during the Baroque

One of the striking hallmarks of the Baroque derives from design techniques that extend to the very borders of illusion, and also from the use of optically deceptive materials, especially in interior design. When one steps into a Baroque or Rococo building, such as the main church of the Benedictine

[114] The interior of the monastery church at Ottobeuren, Germany: an example of interior decor of the late Baroque (1st half of the 18th century.)

103

[115] Balthasar Neumann. Tiepolo's portrait of the master builder in a ceiling fresco in the Würzburg Residence.

monastery at Ottobeuren in southern Germany (114), the visitor is almost overpowered by the magnificence of the design with its ornamentation. Various colored marbles, relief work, gleaming metallic ornamentation and deceptively exact painting fill, and even overfill, the eye. Only someone who approaches such typically Baroque decoration more closely will detect the disguises at work. There is no real marble; instead, artfully painted wooden paneling is the dominating element of design. The precisely chiseled reliefs and details of the architectural ornamentation reveal themselves to be painted plaster or wooden carvings, just as what seem to be metallic elements are in reality plaster either coated with metal-based paint, or at most gilded with an extremely thin layer of gold leaf or a minimal amount of silver. These materials, so imposing from a distance, reveal their "crude" and earthy origins upon closer examination. Tricks of perspective and application of paint designed to work at a distance are the techniques behind these *trompe-l'oeil* effects.

Naturally, there are also numerous Baroque buildings in which these decorative details are "real"—that is, at least made out of the actual materials that in Ottobeuren seem to leap so strikingly to the eye. And yet, contemporary judgment barely made a distinction between the "real" thing and a successful imitation. As with the *trompe-l'oeil* techniques in painting, so in architecture: Art consisted in the optically deceptive imitation, for which patrons were often willing to pay more than for similar decor executed in the actual materials. The Baroque produced numerous famed works that are masterpieces of these deceptive techniques. Outstanding masters of the techniques in the southern German Baroque tradition include the Wessobrunner stucco workers, in particular Mathias Schmuzer and his son Johann (2nd half of the 17th century) and the school that arose around them (including Johannes Schütz, and the Winkler and Üblher families, 1st half of the 18th century).

The success of these Baroque disguises in the interiors of buildings depended on sophisticated and well-thought-out lighting. Churches, as well as most of the impressive secular buildings of the Baroque, are provided with copious daylight by means of both visible windows and other openings that at first may not be apparent to the eye. Particular value was laid on side lighting which, because of the spatial depth of the rooms, produced light and shadow effects that further emphasized the relief character of the ornamentation. In fact, because of this concern for optimal lighting, it was often the direction of the sun rather than traditional strictures of Western architecture that determined the geographical orientation of a building.

A similar decorative impulse can be seen in the form and design of the exterior ornamentation of bourgeois houses. The decorations may well be proof against the elements, but are nonetheless not "real" in the material sense. Such city houses enabled the

[116] In Prague: Baroque facades line a city square.

prosperous, essentially non-aristocratic, middle class to present itself as an economic, if not political or social, elite. Surviving examples of such Baroque city landscapes can be found in the Italian Tyrol, for example, in Bolzano or in Prague (116).

The three great palaces: El Escorial, Versailles, and the Reggia of Caserta

Alongside of church architecture, the building of palaces stands as the high point of secular architecture during the Baroque period. Three great palaces—El Escorial near Aranjuez in Spain, Versailles outside of Paris, and the Reggia of Caserta near Naples—must be considered exemplary works. If El Escorial, built in the 16th century, may be seen as the bud of the movement, Versailles (17th century) is the full-blown flower, and Caserta (18th century)

[117] An exemplary early Baroque palace: El Escorial near Madrid.

the fading flower of the Baroque princely residence. Although such an approach is plausible in certain aspects, it does pose great formal problems in the way of a full understanding of such palaces.

Architectural complexes such as these are neither solely nor primarily to be seen as works of art, and thereby described in terms intrinsic to artistic phenomena; instead, they must be considered in a social-historical perspective. From such a perspective, El Escorial, Versailles, and the Reggia of Caserta are identical in at least one respect: They are gigantic, exaggerated trophies of absolutist stamp. In relation to the real needs of the people of the time, they represent an immense waste of labor, material, and landscape for the sake of creating a stage setting for the scenes of courtly life played out by the nobility. Spurred by boundless opportunity, the nobility competed with each other in protestations of loyalty and honor toward the king, and lived largely on fiefs granted by the crown—that is, at the cost of others, doing little more than extorting fees and dues from the land and from the peasant population in as flagrant a manner as possible. In this sense, the Reggia of Caserta does not represent a decline at all, but just the opposite. It may even be the unsurpassed high point of the absolutist pirate mentality. Delicate description with a finely chiseled art-historical vocabulary—even if it addresses architectural realities in an immediate sense—is thoroughly capable of losing sight of these social-historical aspects in favor of comparatively super-ficial art terms.

Construction on El Escorial (117), the castle built by Philip II south of Madrid as a display of magni-ficence, began in 1563. The architects were Juan Bautista de Toledo, who had already successfully renovated Naples (then under Spanish control), and Francisco de Herrera (ca. 1530–1597), who succeeded Toledo upon his death in 1567. In comparison to the complexes at Versailles and Caserta in the centuries following, El Escorial was laid out on a comparatively modest, nearly square ground plan about 656 feet on each side. The four wings arranged around an inner court served very different functions. El Escorial was not purely a princely castle, but a combination of royal residence and monastery in which the religious areas actually dominated. The royal chambers, oriented to the garden rather than to the front, constituted hardly more than an annex to the central church. This unique union of sacred and impressive worldly architecture irrefutably demonstrates the close interweaving of religious and secular power in 16th century Spain.

Versailles, initiated by Louis XIV in 1661 on the site of a small water-palace dating from the early 17th century, would become the much-copied prototype of the Baroque castle. Based on the plans of Louis Le Vau, a gigantic architectural stage arose in successive phases around an already existent "ideal city" (118). Behind the almost 2000-foot-wide front, the u-shaped central area of the palace was flanked by two broad wings. In other words, unlike El Escorial, Versailles was not oriented around a central rectangle. The wings framing the courtyard stretched back more than 1,300 feet, creating a structure of previously unheard of dimensions—a building which still today overwhelms the observer and credibly underscores the motto of Louis XIV: *L'etat c'est moi* ("I am the state"). The palace was combined with a huge garden area begun in 1667 under Le Nôtre. The park, which was laid out along ruler-line straight lines in a typical French drawing board style (see page 112), in the end consumed almost 2 square miles of the surrounding landscape.

[118] Absolutist design: The "ideal city" of Versailles (foreground), the immense royal palace (middle), and the precisely laid-out garden (rear). Copper engraving ca. 1700. Illustrations such as these helped the planning of the palatial building project at Karlsruhe (on the middle Rhine), which was a copy of this image of Versailles on a smaller scale.

Almost all attempts by other absolutist princes of the Baroque period to surpass Versailles failed. In some respects an exception to the rule, however, was the princely residence of the Bourbon ruler Charles III in Caserta near Naples. Intended as a replacement

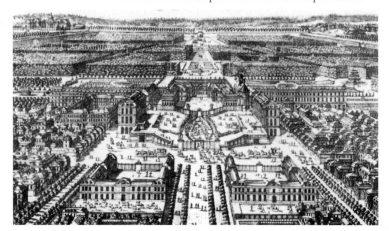

for the "city palace" in Naples that had been built between 1752 and 1774 under the direction of Luigi Van-vitelli, the new, almost square ground plan of the palace at Caserta is reminiscent of El

[119]   The heart of the palace. The center of a princely Baroque residence such as that at Caserta was the magnificent theatrical staircase, where important elements of courtly ceremony were played out before the eyes of the aristocracy.

Escorial. With a facade of almost 980 feet, however, it is considerably larger than the Spanish palace. Although the palace at Caserta lacks the extremely long side wings of Versailles (the wings encompassing the courtyard of El Escorial were added in the late 17th century), Caserta surpassed the palace of the French Sun King in various "important" details, according to contemporary records: the number of windows (1,742), the number of chimneys rising from the roof (1,026), the number of rooms (1,200), and finally, the length, if not the total area, of the garden (almost 2.5 miles).

In the shadow of magnificence: Timber frame houses and inhabited bridges

The timber frame house (sometimes loosely known as "Tudor style"), with its walls filled out with a woven wooden gridwork, clay or bricks, is the product of a greater or lesser shortage of wood in various areas, and has offered a useful building technique since antiquity. It may seem surprising at first to place this

[120] City timber-frame house of the "little people" along the Quai de la Poissonnerie on the outskirts of Colmar in Alsace, France, early 18th century.

type of building under the shadow of magnificence, but beginning in the 15th century, timber frame building in large parts of Germany, Alsace, Normandy, southern England, and the Balkans underwent a renaissance. Numerous impressive buildings were constructed in this style, including homes of the wealthy bourgeois and city halls (Melsungen near Kassel, Esslingen and Lüneburg, all in Germany), with gables and other compartmented wall areas richly decorated with carved wood. Entire city landscapes (Chester and York in England, Goslar in Germany) have survived to define the image of timber-frame houses as a form of urban architecture of the 16th and 17th centuries meant to impress the onlooker.

The urban bourgeois pomp offered by timber-frame construction should not be allowed to disguise the original country origin of this building style, however. Initially, it was the cottages of poor peasants or fisherfolk that were constructed in this basically simple and, above all, inexpensive technique—usually with no ornamentation and only a few windows—based on a crooked wooden framework that was quickly filled in with clay and daub. Furthermore, the 17th and 18th centuries were marked by a flight from the countryside to the cities, resulting in a second kind of timber-frame construction. In many of the timber-frame towns with their splendid public and private timber-frame buildings, there were also numerous small, low-ceilinged, crooked timber-frame cottages—today a quaint subject for photographs—which were hastily built outside the city centers. These formed in a sense a new suburb of simple dwellings for the common people.

In the 16th and 17th centuries, enormous expansion of the urban population greatly increased the population density in the large cities, and led to an ever more glaring lack of space for building. One result of this compression was the phenomenon of inhabited bridges, which could be found in almost all larger cities of the age (121). Houses were built on both sides of the bridge, almost as if perched on a cliff. Often four or five stories high, these light constructions were susceptible at any moment to collapse and were constantly threatened by fire. Here, in the midst of the noisy traffic, lived the poor of the city. The images that today seem so picturesque, or descriptions of "living" bridges that were found in great numbers, especially in Paris and London, distort the reality of housing arising out of direst need that by today's standards was extremely narrow, noisy, and depressing.

[121] "Living" bridge: the Pont du Change in Paris. Painting by Nicolas and Jean-Baptiste Raguenet, 1758. Musée Carnavalet, Paris. Due to acute structural problems, the five-story brick buildings were razed after 1786.

From Dinocrates to Borromeo:

[122] The absolutely straight Roman tunnel dating from the 1st century AD connected Naples with the Via Comitiana, the road leading from the harbors of Miseno, Puteoli, and Baiae to Rome. The tunnel remained in use into the 19th century. Painting by A. Sminck Pittoo, 19th c. Rijksmuseum, Amsterdam.

One of the hallmarks of the Baroque is its rigorous treatment of nature. Whether in the construction of buildings or the layout of gardens, during the Baroque period the transformation of reality gradually took on the character of a cultural mandate that expressed the unqualified dominance of humanity and its accomplishments over nature. This understanding of human omnipotence was already a comprehensive philosophy in the ancient classical world. The Hellenistic architect Dinocrates's idea to transform Mount Athos into an immense image of Alexander the

Great, and thus allow the Macedonian king to hold in his hand an entire city with all its inhabitants, is a reflection of this tradition (136).

The urge to reform nature is also particularly striking in Roman villa architecture, with its complex intellectual and formal connections between landscapes and buildings. Villas were ideally located on sites that offered a broad view of the surrounding landscape. The importance of this position is underlined by the efforts taken to create a panoramic landscape when no "natural" one was available: Many villas were constructed on artificial terraces or platforms built for that purpose. The view of the surrounding countryside was further tied to the organization of the rooms; scenes of nature were captured and framed by the architecture. In this way, the rooms functioned almost like a series of theater curtains designed to frame imposing panoramas, which were often extended and elaborated upon by means of carefully placed openings and illusionistic wall paintings framing the windows.

At the same time, the landscape itself was integrated into the functional concept of the villa—in the form of an artificial creation when the natural surroundings were unfavorable. Gardens were equipped with man-made hills; ponds were laid out without consideration of the suitability of the terrain (even hewn into rock at times); grottoes, artificial if necessary, were pressed into service as dining rooms; rocky ledges were used to provide shade; creeks —often with redirected courses—burbled through the landscape. In this manner, nature was "perfected" and made into an idealized component of culture—a striking instance of the militancy of the Roman attitude toward nature. Roman engineers completely subjugated the earth, moved or tunneled though mountains (122), bridged valleys and rivers, laid out roads in direct lines through the landscape, dried swamps, and proclaimed themselves the rulers and improvers of the world through their accomplishments.

The ancient classical idea of nature as a malleable substance was taken up again by the Baroque era and intensified in an extremely eccentric manner. A famous example, much admired in its age, was the renovation of Isola Bella island in Lake Maggiore (123) under Charles III Borromeo in the mid-17th century. In the process, the once unremarkable island was robbed entirely of its natural character and refashioned into a kind of ship-palace. The contours of the island, once a flat boulder, were cut into a long rectangle. With im-

mense effort, the landscape was then terraced by transporting the soil from one place to another, and the whole was then transformed into a garden-island, crowned by a palace that in places reached up to ten stories. In the end the island resembled a megalomaniac artificially "natural" ship lying at anchor.

Particular evidence of the Baroque love of reformed nature is also to be found in the artfully designed gardens commonly known as "French gardens" because of their first appearance in France during the 16th century. The hallmark of these gardens were geometrically shaped beds and rows of trees and sculpted hedges; artificial creeks complete with cascades, pools, springs, and fountains; and carefully planned graveled walks. One of the most important garden architects of the Baroque was Andre Le Nôtre (1613–1700), a protégé of Louis XIV. Among his many projects was the park at Versailles, designed with the aid of the same kind of minutely detailed plans that would be used for a building.

[123] Isola Bella ("beautiful island") in Lake Maggiore after being refashioned into a ship-palace. Etching from the early 19th century.

Architecture in the process of change: "Revolutionary" architecture

The architectural historian Emil Kaufmann coined the term "revolutionary architecture" in the 1930s. He was not referring to a clearly defined architectural epoch; instead, his term characterizes the far-reaching architectural innovations of the late 18th century—not only those of France in the throes of revolution. The front-line protagonists of this architecture of the revolutionary age were primarily Frenchmen such as Claude-Nicolas Ledoux (1736–1806) and Etienne-Louis Boullée, but the term also includes such German early classicists as Friedrich Weinbrenner (1766–1818) and Friedrich Gilly (1772–1800).

Architecture of the revolutionary age placed its faith on two basically antithetical principles, a forward-looking utopia and a retrospective classicism, holding both in fine theoretical balance. This architecture has less to do with the actual realization or construction of buildings than with architectural theory; it exists primarily in designs and concepts. It forms a counterweight to Baroque absolutism (see page 100) without being entirely disconnected from it. The formal dependence of revolutionary architecture on Greco-Roman design is anchored in the Baroque, especially as practiced in France. The overriding goal was to produce eloquent architecture, expressive buildings whose designs were immediately evident to the viewer. In this sense, the architecture of the revolutionary age was not completely new. The French architects Ledoux and Boullée were rooted just as much in the French absolutism of the decades preceding 1789 as in the academic concept of an *architecture parlante*. Accordingly, the classification of revolutionary architecture as well as the *oeuvre* of individual architects still hovers between late Baroque and early (neo-)classical influences.

Unlike the ornamental playfulness of Baroque, architecture of the revolutionary age is concerned with the realization of a rationally motivated and precise geometry. This was the basis for designs that still seem futuristic today. Boullée, for example, designed a cenotaph as a monument to his idol, the physicist Sir Isaac Newton (124), in pre-revolutionary Paris of 1784. It was to take the form of a huge sphere: Behind the mantled exterior, the hollow interior was filled with cathedral-like fittings. The monument was a concretely demonstrative piece of architecture; Newton, "explainer" of the earth's spherical form, could be celebrated in no more suitable way. This design also made Boullée a forerunner of architectonic megalomania, another characteristic of revolutionary architecture: His sphere was to measure no less than 490 feet in diameter.

In contrast to the works of Boullée, many of the architectural designs of Claude-Nicolas Ledoux, which present an exemplary mixture of early classical utopianism and *architecture parlante*, were actually built. Several of his early works (including the court facade of the Hôtel d'Uzès, Paris) are firmly anchored in the Baroque; but from the 1770s utopian conceptions became more prominent, as seen in his proposal for an ideal city at the salt works Salines de Chaux at Arc-et-Senans (125), built largely according to his plans.

Friedrich Gilly's design for a national monument to Frederick the Great subscribes formally to the geometric-utopian principles of revolutionary architecture. In terms of content, however, Gilly reflects the anti-absolutist ideas of his day. It was during these decades that the classical Greek temple was "rediscovered" in the form of the Parthenon. In Gilly's plans, just such a temple rises on a high, authoritative substructure. It is a paragon of German classicism, celebrating the power of the ruling class and averse to any "revolutionary" content (126). By contrast, the design of the Swedish architect Carl August Ehrensvärd

1859–1860
Italian wars of unification lead to national state under King Victor Emanuel II in 1861
1861–1865
American Civil War; abolition of slavery in 1863
1870–1871
Franco-Prussian War; proclamation of German Empire in Versailles

[124]   Etienne-Louis Boullée: design for the cenotaph in honor of Sir Isaac Newton. Exterior view, sketch from 1784.

[125]   Claude-Nicolas Ledoux: entrance gate to the salt-mining city of Chaux (built 1773–1778). Engraving of actual buildings, ca. 1810.

(1745–1800) for the portal of a Karlskrona shipyard spanned by a colossal Doric capsill seems light-hearted and playful (127).

The architecture of the revolutionary age exerted considerable influence: With its megalomaniac tendencies and precise rationality, it later contributed to the totalitarian architectural conceptions of the German National Socialists (Nazis), Italian Fascists, and the Soviet avant-garde. Utopian concepts were decisive in the forms and functional principles of such diverse feats of architectural engineering as the Eiffel Tower and the rocket launching pads of Cape Kennedy. The principle of *architecture parlante*, as formulated by the pioneer Ledoux, also came to be expressed in shortened, squat Doric columns. The heavy, "burdened" colonnade above the vaulted entrances to 19th century prisons and court houses was a metaphor for the oppression suffered by delinquents sent "beneath the yoke" (for example, the entrance to the women's prison of Würzburg by Peter Speeth, 1810).

[126] Friedrich Gilly: national monument to Frederick the Great, design from 1796. The title of a Nazi architectural periodical from 1942 argued the importance of the conception of revolutionary age architecture for the representational needs of the National Socialist Party.

[127] Carl August Ehrensvärd: Portal for a shipyard in the Baltic harbor of Karlskrona. Colored wooden model from 1785. Karlskrona, Maritime Museum.

The rediscovery of Greece: James Stuart and the Greek Revival

Since the early Renaissance, architecture of the ancient classical world had provided the overriding paradigm for contemporary building and the basis for theoretical discussions of architecture (see page 84, 98). The established image of classical architecture, however, took into account only one episode of the age, namely the well-known and oft-visited monuments of ancient Rome. In contrast, ancient Greece and its buildings were almost totally unknown. The country itself lay remote from the centers of the Ottoman Empire and was for all intents and purposes out of bounds for travelers. Explorations began in the 18th century, motivated by the Enlightenment's enthusiasm for restoring democracy to ancient Greece. The result was the "rediscovery" of Greece, and a corollary rediscovery of "purely" Greek architectural forms and paradigms ("pure" in the sense that they were no longer Roman). These discoveries quickly entered the architectural landscape of the 18th and 19th centuries.

Discovery of three well-preserved Doric temples at Paestum in southern Italy marked the starting point. Once the pride of a Greek colonial city, the temples had been hidden for centuries in an overgrown swamp until they were found by chance in the 1740s. For the first time, Greek Doric architecture appeared before the eyes of the modern world: The original form of this architectural order had found no practical resonance in ancient Roman architecture, and was thus quite unknown to subsequent ages. Two competing expeditions to Greece increased this new knowledge. The Frenchman LeRoy traveled through Greece in 1755; his book, *Les Ruines de plus beaux Monuments de la Grèce*, filled with detailed drawings, appeared in 1758 and caused a worldwide sensation. The expedition of two English architects, James Stuart and Nicholas Revett, was considerably more thorough. Sponsored by the London Society of Dilettanti in 1750, the two men were to make a detailed list of antique buildings in Athens and Attica. The splendid, elaborately illustrated folio, *Antiquities of Athens* (128), was the product of a journey lasting several years. Due to technical difficulties, the individual volumes of the work were not immediately available, but appeared at long intervals between 1762 and 1816.

James Stuart is not only associated with the exploration of ancient Greek architecture, but also with the adaptation of original classical Greek building forms by

[128] Columns and entablature of the Erechtheion on the Athenian Acropolis (late 5th century BC) as a paradigmatic example of Greek Ionic architecture. Plate from Stuart's and Revett's *Antiquities of Athens* (1787).

Classicism and Historicism: The Rediscovery of Greece

[129] American Greek Revival architecture: the facade of the old patent office in Washington D.C. (Robert Mills, architect, built 1836–1840). The entrance is ornamented with a Doric temple front boasting eight columns, modeled on the Parthenon on the Acropolis, Athens. Daguerrotype from 1846.

contemporary architecture. "Greek Revival" as an architectural concept had its beginnings in Stuart's early works (such as the garden temples at Hagley Park, 1759, and Shugborough Park, 1761). Moreover, ancient Greek buildings were immediately and widely accepted by a society which saw them as symbols of concerns at the heart of the Enlightenment: human dignity and the love of freedom. Stuart himself, who was known as "Athenian Stuart" for his love of classical Doric and Ionic forms, became the model and inspiration for an entire generation of architects who set out to adorn all of England and Scotland with buildings in the classical Greek style.

The detailed drawings of the ancient Greek orders published in the 18th century quickly found their way into the design books and plans of American architects, where the Greek forms enhanced the classicism that had been practiced since Thomas Jefferson (1743–1826). Like the work of French architects Gabriel (1698–1772) and Soufflot (1713–1780), it was oriented toward ancient Rome and the Italian Renaissance. This striking mixture of styles formulated a real alternative to the architecture of the English enemy during the War of Independence. The features of American Greek Revival in the decades before 1860 are found in government and administrative buildings (129), and especially the stately homes of prominent citizens, which were an important outward expression of their economic prosperity and social status.

In its devotion to the architecture of ancient Greece, the Greek Revival initiated 19th century classicism. Today, a modern form of neoclassicism is also based on this late 18th and early 19th-century development. The modern movement, mainly an American phenomenon

Important architects of the English Greek Revival include:
John Soane (1753–1837)
Robert Smirke (1780–1876)
John Nash (1752–1835)
and the Scots
William Playfair (1790–1857)
Thommas Hamilton (1784–1858)
Alexander Thomson (1817–75)

(130), purports to "endow [buildings] with meaning," and thus stands in opposition to the seeming confusions of post-modernism (see page 171).

Schinkel and Klenze: Classicism in Prussia and Bavaria

In the Anglo-Saxon world, Greek Revival was intimately connected to such concerns as the rights of free citizens and a democratic, parliamentary form of government. The rediscovery of classical Greek architecture in Greece also manifested itself in Prussia and Bavaria, where it also became an eagerly emulated ideal. Nevertheless, in Germany, classicism soon mutated from a futuristic vision (as formulated in Herder's "Plastik," for example) to a reactionary form, a vehicle for an authoritarian, monarchic display of power. The Greek forms and orders were ideally suited for this use. What arose in Prussia and Bavaria under the banner of classicism were nationalistic government buildings and monuments to statesmen, buildings that were meant to impress on the people the dignity and virtue of their rulers, the permanence of the monarchy, and the eternal greatness of the nation. The newly discovered Doric order, with its lack of ornamentation and seemingly indestructible tectonic form, seemed best suited to this purpose .

Friedrich Schinkel (1781–1841) was the main figure of Prussian classicism. Trained at the Berlin Bauakademie under the direction of Friedrich Gilly, Schinkel came into early contact not only with the "pure" formal dogma of classicism, but also with the utopian-like concepts of revolutionary-age architecture. At first Schinkel had no success as an architect, but his talent as a painter and stage set designer guaranteed a good income. His architectural *oeuvre* began only in 1816 when, as protégé of Wilhelm von Humboldt, he was

[130] Greek Revival? Contemporary American neoclassicism: the Doric entrance portal to Johnston & Wales University, Watertown, Massachusetts. Imai & Keller Architects Inc., 1994

Important architects of the American Greek Revival include:
Benjamin H. Latrobe (1764–1820)
William Strickland (1787–1854)

granted a position by the Prussian building authorities. He became the head of the department in 1830. Schinkel's early works, especially the Neue Wache, the Altes Museum, and the theater on the Gendarmenmarkt in Berlin, mirror the classicist "law and order" mentality of the monarchy, which formed itself anew following the Congress of Vienna at the close of the Napoleonic wars. These buildings became symbols of Prussia's return to national grandeur. Throughout his life, Schinkel remained a "wanderer between worlds," adopting in a utilitarian manner neo-Gothic (see illus. 132) as well as strict Romanesque forms. It is possible to see Schinkel as an early historicist, making use of different architectural styles according to need. In addition to his buildings, numerous designs and plans of his bordering on the fantastic that impressively attest to his versatility and creativity have also been preserved (see page 126).

Leo von Klenze (1784–1864) presents a completely different case. From 1818 on, he was the architectural director at the Bavarian court under Ludwig I. A statesman to the core, he was the unconditional subject to the concerns and person of his king. One special field of endeavor for Klenze's classicism grew out of the close ties between Bavaria and Greece, newly freed from the Turkish yoke. (Interestingly, the Bavarian Otto von Wittelsbach was to become the first Greek king in 1835.) Athens and Munich were the twin centers of Klenze's activity; his architectonic and organizational skills quickly transformed Munich into the "Athens on the Isar." The Propylaeon, the buildings surrounding the Königsplatz, the Hall of Fame, numerous museums and monumental buildings lining major intersections made Munich a metropolis that compared favorably with such European centers as Paris, London, or Berlin. At first a classical approach based on ancient Greece dominated the designs, but Klenze later made use of other historical styles (All Saints Church in a Romanesque-Byzantine style, Ludwig Street buildings in a Renaissance-like style, royal residence in a Florentine style, and the Festival Hall in an antique

Roman style). Other major works by Klenze include the Valhalla near Regensburg built in honor of Bavaria, and the equally nationalistic Liberation Hall near Kehlheim (1839–1851)—all instances of the adaptive possibilities of ancient Greek and Roman architecture. The Valhalla was a copy of the Parthenon on the Acropolis in Athens, the Liberation Hall a copy of Theoderic's mausoleum in Ravenna.

[131]   Leo von Klenze: The Munich Propylaeon at the Königsplatz (built 1846–1862), seen from the west. Painting by Klenze done in 1848. The gateway is a copy of the Propylaea of Mnesicles on the Athenian Acropolis (built ca. 440/430 BC).

Klenze was no less successful in Athens, where he took the reigns firmly in hand, and soon, other likeminded architects with classical leanings were drawn into this area. Their goal was to establish a stately modern capital in as authentic a classical Greek style as possible. Classicists like Friedrich Gärtner, the Danish brothers Hans-Christian and Theofil Hansen, and the Austrian Ernst Ziller were all active here. Klenze was responsible for planning the entire new city of Athens, with its axes and squares to the north of the Acropolis. Klenze's influence is particularly clear on the occasion of a meeting with Schinkel on design. The latter had made plans for a royal castle to be erected on the Acropolis among the ancient ruins. Klenze foiled this idea completely, decreeing the Acropolis to be the province of archaeology, and not a site for new royal palaces. In the face of the grave archaeological errors committed during the "excavation" of the Acropolis in the 19th century, many experts today wish that Schinkel's vision, which would largely have protected the ancient ruins, had become reality.

"Which style should we build in?" Historicism

"Which style should we build in?" This was the provocative title the German architect Heinrich Hübsch (1795–1863) gave to his essay that instigated a momentous debate. Hübsch enumerated just over 50 different historical architectural styles, thereby becoming, if not quite voluntarily, the initiator of a battle of styles—a controversy over the "right, " or proper, building. Historicism, as a historical epoch, replaced classicism. To put it more precisely, historicism reduced classicism to a small element in a universally imitative architecture. Nearly all historical building styles were available and used in the second half of the 19th century. In the process, the original meanings and contexts of a style disappeared more and more as various styles were increasingly mingled and combined at will in one and the same building. Historicism developed into the first age of architectural arbitrariness (postmodernism being the second). The main point of the historicist approach was to have a recognizable historical core to a building. By the end of the century, it was precisely this willful arbitrariness which first the proponents of the *Jugendstil* (also known as *Art Nouveau*) and later those of classic modernism reacted to with élan (see page 142, 144).

One early interest of historicism was the resurrection of the Gothic, at first primarily in England. In the so-called Gothic Revival, Gothic buildings, now thoroughly secular in character but with a sanctifying Gothic aura, mushroomed out of the ground. Notable examples are the Houses of Parliament erected between 1840 and 1888 on the banks of the Thames in London (Charles Berry and Augustus Charles Pugin, architects) and the St. Pancreas Railway Station (built

1868–1874; George Gilbert Scott, architect). In Germany, the neo-Gothic trend also made rapid headway, a famous but late example being the Hamburg Rathaus, built in the 1890s. Karl Friedrich Schinkel himself was an adherent of the neo-Gothic movement and produced numerous designs and painted visions of Gothic buildings (132). On the whole, Gothic forms were profaned through this movement, as they were separated from their original ecclesiastical frame of reference and placed into a secular structural context. This fate was not shared by the Romanesque, however, because during the 19th century, the neo-Romanesque was still mainly limited to contemporary church buildings (for example, the cathedral of Tampere, Finland, built 1902–1907).

A favorite subject for architects involved in historicism were castles and fortresses (see page 73). Here, depending on the wishes of the person commissioning the building, the sky was the limit. Ludwig II of Bavaria, for example, with his romantic, idealized— and at times tasteless—view of the Middle Ages, built the fairy-tale castle Neuschwanstein near Füssen in southern Germany (133). The "real" historical core of the conglomerate that arose between 1869 and 1886 was an actual medieval castle ruin, most of which was removed to make room for the new structure. Another landmark of historicist castle building in Germany is

[132]   Gothic vision of the 19th century: *Dom am Wasser* ("Cathedral on the Water"). Oil on canvas; copy of a lost original painting by Karl Friedrich Schinkel (Berlin, Nationalgalerie.) The painting is based on Schinkel's plans for a neo-Gothic cathedral.

[133] Neuschwanstein, the jewel among the many castles built by Ludwig II of Bavaria ("Mad King Ludwig"). Neuschwanstein is a kind of medieval idyll in a romantic world.

[134] The Royal Pavilion in Brighton, the fairy tale palace of the prince regent, built 1815–1818.

the Renaissance-style city castle of Schwerin, begun in 1844 according to plans by Georg Adolph Demmler and Friedrich August Stüler. Ennobled medievalism with "Teutonic" precision was the guiding principle for numerous other castle reconstructions of the 19th century. Haut Koenigsbourg, for example, in Alsace (France) on a peak of the Vosges mountains near Sélestat is not the perfectly preserved medieval castle that it seems to be from the distance. Instead, it was built in the Wilhelmine era and fitted with every possible comfort according to the plans of the architect Bodo Ebhardt (1865–1945) on the remains of a late medieval structure. Further outstanding examples of historicism are the Paris Opera House, done in a neo-Baroque style (built 1871–1874; Charles Garnier, architect); the "oriental" Royal Pavilion in Brighton (built 1815–1818; John Nash, architect; 134); and the massive Hall of Justice in Brussels, done in classical-Renaissance-like design (built 1866–1883; Joseph Poelaert, architect). The Ringstrasse in Vienna offers almost a complete panorama of historicist architecture, as do the building ensembles of numerous German baths on the Baltic Sea.

To summarize, historicism does not copy for the sake of copying; it is not merely concerned with form. Instead, historicism is goal-oriented, making

use of historical forms for a purpose. The possibility of "dressing up" new buildings in a historical aura was meant to confer age, honor, and tradition where there was none. This was an enticing alternative, especially in new cities, where the lack of traditional historical roots could be camouflaged, feelings of cultural insignificance could be countered, and the course of "real" history shaded or even consciously falsified. Cities which first grew to prominence during the 18th and 19th centuries adorned themselves with "Gothic" town halls or "medieval" timber frame buildings, while the aristocracy, threatened with their own social demise in the 19th century, resuscitated, at least architecturally, the "good old days" in their palaces and urban residences. In the history-less cities of the United States, whole series of "Romanesque" churches arose, as well as capitals in ancient classical or Renaissance outfits.

[135] "Hall of the Lost Steps" in the Palace of Justice in Brussels, Belgium (architect: Joseph Poelaert).

The changing face of glass, iron, and brick

More than any other epoch, the architectural history of the 19th century is characterized by technical innovations, both in terms of building materials and the wider spectrum of structural forms and building techniques that were made possible by these innovations. Iron was the essential raw material not only for architecture, but for the entire process of 19th-century industrialization and mechanization. Beginning in 1709, a coking process made brittle cast iron available, and from about 1850, hardened sectional iron was produced from rolled steel. In iron, architects discovered a practical building material that allowed them to span large distances more simply and economically than previously possible. The bridge at Coalbrookdale in England (1779), built by Englishman Abraham Darby, is considered the first piece of iron architecture. Ever bolder and lighter constructions followed in quick succession, often in the neo-Gothic style. The most outstanding monument to the iron construction of the 19th century is the more than 980-foot-high Eiffel Tower constructed for the World Exposition of 1889 in

[136] Johann Berhard Fischer von Erlach: Vision of the ancient architect Dinocrates's Athos project. From *Plans for a historical architecture*, 1721, plate XVIII.

Ideal architecture in an ideally created landscape—this is a concept that has tantalized visionary architects, painters, and poets not only during the romantic era of the 19th century, but with almost equal ardor throughout the ages. Of course, the idea of a peaceful idyll in the midst of a paradisiacal world was equally often a feature of a despot's totalitarian dream. Architectural visions of this kind existed already in the ancient world, dating back to Dinocrates' idea to turn Mount Athos into a monument to Alexander.

Johann Bernhard Fischer von Erlach (1656–1723), an Austrian Baroque architect, revived this idea and actualized it in the form of a large-format, richly fanciful drawing (136).

Ideal architecture was also a popular motif of ancient Roman wall paintings, which often offered illusionistic views into the distance, views into light-imbued gardens with small architectural structures, or complex views of other fancifully ornamented villas standing in relation to one another. Perhaps the most prominent example is a wall decoration from a villa in Boscoreale near Pompeii (137), part of which today resides in the New York Metropolitan Museum of Art.

Inspired by such architectural fantasies, as well as by the numerous literary and painted fictions of the Renaissance and the Baroque, effective visualization of utopian

[137] Wall painting from a villa that was buried by Vesuvius, in Boscoreale. The illusionist fresco, once combined with a view of an actual natural landscape, shows its own context: the villa as an ideal life. Second Pompeii style, ca. 50 BC.

The Idea of Pure Happiness--Utopian Architectural Fancies

buildings became an important field of endeavor for the architects of the classically oriented Romanticism of the 19th century. Without much material expenditure, they could demonstrate their academic knowledge and technical skill, as well as an entire range of individual ideas and concepts, in painting. The Prussian Karl-Friedrich Schinkel (see page 119) was a master of such architectural fantasies,

book *Werke der höheren Baukunst* (*Works of Higher Architecture*); the other buildings illustrated were in fact realized. The climax of such a classical-romantic approach was Schinkel's painting of a romantic utopia with an ancient classical temple. Although the original has not been preserved, a precise copy made by Wilhelm Ahlborn exists.

Despite their rivalries, the Bavarian Leo von Klenze and Schinkel

[138]   Leo von Klenze, *Athen im Altertum (Athens of Old)*, painting from 1862.

vacillating between the romantic perspectives of a Caspar David Friedrich and Schinkel's own, realized building conceptions. His ideas for a royal palace on the Acropolis in Athens and the palace for the czar near Orianda on the Crimean peninsula, worked out in plans and detailed views, were never built. Nevertheless, they are at the center of Schinkel's 1845

were soulmates. Klenze's ornate painting "Athen im Altertum" (138) forms a contrast to Schinkel's enthusiastic conception of the Acropolis palace in its historicizing, antique approach. Nevertheless, Klenze's painting, envisioning an ideal past rather than an idealized present, is just as subject to the romantic-utopian vision as Schinkel's palace.

Paris. Despite considerable opposition to his plan, Gustave Eiffel completed his work, which became the new landmark of Paris and was named after its maker (139). Iron increased in practical importance and became ever more widely used in the construction of bridges and later for high-rise buildings.

A further possibility opened up when a sleek but robust iron skeleton was combined with glass surfaces—a principle that had already been used in the construction of large-surface windows in Gothic cathedrals. The numerous glass-and-iron constructions of the 19th century made use of this model, resulting in modern "cathedrals," flooded with light, with wide arches and vaults. By traditional standards, the frame of such buildings appears so minimal and fragile that the entire structure seems to float; in fact, in terms of structural engineering, the buildings are exceedingly sturdy.

[139] The Eiffel Tower of Paris (built 1889).

One of the first types of buildings architects turned their attention to was orangeries and greenhouses in parks and large gardens, where form and practical purpose were inseparable. The Crystal Palace in London epitomized the desire to display the technical possibilities of glass-and-iron buildings. This was "recreational" architecture at its best: a giant, complexly partitioned exhibition hall rising to a height of 72 feet stretched over an area of nearly 2.5 acres, and offering all kinds of enjoyments. Built by Joseph Paxton (1801–1855) in Hyde Park for the London World Exhibition of 1852, the Crystal Palace was later dismantled and rebuilt in the Sydenham section of the city, wholly in keeping with the 19th-century mania for innovation and its appreciation of the technically doable. Here the Palace remained until its destruction by fire in 1936. Paxton's modular form of construction was revolutionary. The Crystal Palace was built of only a few prefabricated standard parts, whose size was determined by a grid that was maintained through the entire building. In this case, the ability of the new building material to serve rational production was effectively

[140] London, the Crystal Palace. Plan for the interior decor by Owen Hones (1850). The three-aisled, light-flooded "basilica" received its now-accepted name from the satirical magazine *Punch*, which used the term derisively in November 1851.

demonstrated. The London model found many imitators; many cities, including New York, Munich, and Paris, saw the rise of similar "glass palaces."

The third technical-aesthetic innovation in the architecture of the 19th century was already widely used both in ancient Rome and again during the Gothic period, namely brick. During the 19th century, bricks not only served the historicist-romantic interest in "material honesty" in construction; but as a pre-fabricated, machine-produced building technology, brick offered technical possibilities comparable to those provided by iron-and-glass combinations. Although brick and glass are two completely different materials, they are ideally suited to be combined in filling out an architectural framework made of iron. Their use became standard, forming the basis for the almost unlimited forms of 19th-century architecture. Some of the buildings that arose seemed at the time to be sheerly impossible from the point of view of structural engineering—brick buildings on iron frames with boldly constructed glass roofs flooding the interior with light. Large market halls, shopping arcades (141), and railway stations and industrial buildings (see page 138)—these are the prototypes of the new form of architecture. Moreover, the technique of iron framing made a great contribution to the development of high-rise buildings (see page 132). Although these structures were belittled for a long time as common and ordinary, they have recently been rediscovered as historical monuments, and many of them—not so very durable after all—have been restored and preserved from decay.

[141] The Galleria Umberto I. In the heart of Naples (built 1887–1890). Its light, wide roof construction of iron and glass is, together with the Galleria Vittorio Emanuele II (built 1865–1867) in Milan, the most prominent example of Italian arcade architecture of the 19th century.

129

Architecture Competitions

Often, architecture competitions seem a rather modern invention. With their clear objectives in terms of finance, construction, and design, the organization of such contests is orderly, almost bureaucratic, and the roles of the commissioner of the building, the organizers of the competition, the jury, and the competing participants seem to be clear. Actually, however, such orderly competitions for announced projects have existed since ancient times. In the democratic Athens of the 5th and 4th centuries BC, public buildings were a matter for the *polis*, the city state. A convocation of the populace might decide to build a temple, for example. They then formulated objectives for the appearance and cost of the building, had various architects submit plans, and then made their selection by vote. The actual construction was allotted to a "building committee," which in turn was responsible for the financing, the task-oriented description of the various kinds of work involved and the standards for proper execution, and finally, if necessary, for collecting the fines for breach of contract.

The history of modern architectural competitions can be dated to the beginning of the 15th century. At this time in Florence, different architects were asked to submit ideas for a dome for the city's cathedral. The plan submitted by Filippo Brunelleschi (1377–1446) won and was realized between 1419 and 1436.

Nevertheless, architecture competitions came to be common practice only at the beginning of the 18th century. At that time, competitions were more concerned with the basic idea or design; today, competitions tend to emphasize the technical possibilities for the realization of the building. The objective of the traditional contests was for the initiator of the project (usually a government or communal commissioner, and only rarely a private individual) to acquire a comprehensive package of suggestions (the basic idea had already been formulated) as to the structural design of the proposed project. Then as now, the competition might be either opened or closed. When open, no limit is set as to the number of participants; when closed, plans are accepted only from participants chosen and contacted in advance.

The competitiveness of individual architects in such competitions is to a large extent dependent on their ability to present ideas and concepts to a jury or other decision-making body as a visual structural model. The architectural model, especially the imaginary-illusionist, large-format drawing offering various views, became instrumental in the success of a submitted plan. Brunelleschi, for example, had made a wooden model of his plan for the cathedral of Florence that presented essential features of his concept better than a mere drawing could have. Many drawings from the major architecture competitions of the late 18th and 19th centuries have been preserved, including some of special interest to the history of architecture like plans for the White House in Washington D.C. (1792), Valhalla near Regensburg (1814), the Houses of Parliament in London (1835/36), the Paris Opera House (1861), and the Reichstag in Berlin (1872/82). Even drawings for plans that were not selected and were never built are interesting and today supplement our understanding of this architectural age.

In the case of the Valhalla (142), Carl von Fischer's design proposed a domed central-plan building in the style of the Pantheon in Rome. According to the stipulations of the competition, the Greek Doric order was to be used as a sign of dignified gravity, so Fischer placed a temple portico with eight Doric columns in front of this domed structure. This design was, in fact, a reversion to the Parthenon on the Athenian Acropolis, which Leo von Klenze's winning design also employed. But Fischer's citation of the Parthenon was not exclusive; in his plan the Parthenon and the Pantheon were homogeneously united. The extent to which the architectural stipulations of the organizers or commissioners can influence or even limit the plans submitted can also be seen in the example of the Reichstag in Berlin. The plan submitted by architects Hermann Ende and Wilhelm Böckmann, surprisingly enough, mirrors in all essential structures the plan and conception of Paul Wallot, which was chosen and built.

Architecture competitions are common practice for nearly all large building projects today, and the process is legally regulated in almost all countries. However, this does not exclude arguments and public discussions about these projects, as could be recently witnessed in debate about Sir Norman Foster's plans for the renovation of the Reichstag in Berlin or in the debate over Daniel Liebeskind's plans for the Jewish Museum in Berlin. Numerous architecture magazines offer information about different competitions and their stipulations. In addition to these competitions for projects that are intended to be realized, since the 19th century there have been increasing numbers of prizes purely for architecture design, offering creative architects another platform through which they can develop and present their unique visions.

[142] Carl von Fischer: Plan for Valhalla near Regensburg, Bavaria, ca. 1809/10.

Chicago architecture:
The genesis of the skyscraper

Disasters and mishaps have more than once provided important impulses in the history of architecture and community building development. The fire of Rome in AD 64, the London and Hamburg conflagrations of 1666 and 1842 respectively, and the San Francisco earthquake and fire of 1909 were all events that, beyond the tragedy of human loss and destruction, led to large-scale reconstruction of the cities according to the latest standards, and thus also to architectural innovation.

In 19th century America, apart from the east coast metropolises, Chicago was the most important crossroads for trade and traffic between the east and west coasts and thus one of the most quickly and radically expanding cities in the United States. Its booming economy lured people to the city, which between 1850 and 1870 experienced a population explosion from barely 30,000 to more than 300,000, becoming for a time by far the largest city in the United States. The conflagration that left almost the complete inner city in ashes and ruins in 1871 came as a great shock.

The Chicago that emerged as a result of an enormous expenditure of energy after the fire became a synonym for architectural modernity, giving impulse to a pragmatic "American" method of building. There was a considerable lack of land within the relatively small inner city area. In addition, the immense demand for commercial and office space far exceeded the supply. Building vertically was the only possible solution to these problems. Thus, structures were required that not only provided numerous stories for offices but, with rows of shop windows and arcades facing the streets, also offered an airy design for business and presentation purposes. These requirements constituted an insoluble engineering problem for the conservative building methods of the day. The iron (later steel) beam skeleton developed in England around 1840 offered the solution that Chicago needed in the 1870s. Metal beams formed the frame for wall areas that would be filled in with brick. Leroy S. Buffington became a pioneer in this technology by altering and improving the English model, and soon held numerous patents for high-rise metal-framed buildings whose stable but light construction based on securely connected T- and I-beams could reach more than 25 stories in height (143). In the 1880s, the many-storied office buildings that were to become Chicago's hallmark sprang from the earth on almost every street corner in the heart of the city. Such buildings consisted of a steel or iron skeleton; a facade with many windows, whether richly or sparsely decorated; a splendid top floor with a flat roof; an optically distinguished ground floor that could also be used for formal presentations; and finally, a lordly *piano nobile*, or smaller, richly decorated chamber to be used for special purposes.

This "Chicago architecture" forthwith became the model for other American metropolises facing the same urban problems: too little space "close in;" access to city utilities; and a great need for renovation. The high-rise building became the decisive architectural form of rational, capital- and

1924
Death of Lenin, power struggle between Trotsky and Stalin in Russia
after 1929
Creation and consolidation of USSR under Stalin
1933
Adolf Hitler elected German chancellor, end of Weimar Republic, beginning of Nazi dictatorship

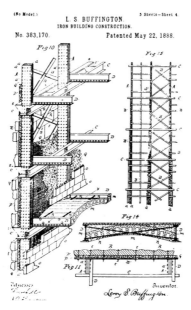

[143] Page 4 of the five-page patent application for Leroy S. Buffington's "Iron Building Construction," granted on May 22, 1888. The application discusses the optimizing of horizontal and vertical stresses in high-rise construction and asserts the enormous load-carrying capacity of T-beams.

[144] William LeBaron Jenney: Home Insurance Building, on the corner of LaSalle and Adams Street in Chicago, built in 1884. View from 1897. The epoch-making building, which was the first true skyscraper in Chicago, was razed in the 1930s.

trade-oriented modern design—and remains so today. The essence of space-saving multi-story architecture is now found in Manhattan, whose legendary skyscrapers were tremendously influenced, both formally and technically, by the developments in Chicago. Just how eagerly every opportunity to erect a spectacular skyscraper was grasped can be seen by the example of the Fuller Flatiron Building (146), built by Damsel Hudson Burnham in 1902—a monumental 20-story building on a steel framework standing on an extremely narrow, triangular lot at the intersection of Broadway and Fifth Avenue.

High-rise buildings of all kinds would not be conceivable without two further American inventions—the elevator and air-conditioning, both developments of the 19th century parallel to the multistory building. A *sine qua non* of every building with more than six stories, the mechanical elevator developed by Elisha Graves Otis and presented for the first time in 1857 was driven by a spiral spring technology. The more modern, electric elevator suffered from a bad image for many years because of numerous accidents and falls, but today's (much-improved) ubiquitous model is found around the world (The name of the original inventor lives on in the elevator firm of Flohr & Otis). The term "air conditioning" is derived from a system for "artificial

[145] View down State Street from Washington Street, Chicago. In the center is the Reliance Building, built in 1895 by Daniel Hudson Burnham. Photo from 1928.

weather" in high-rise buildings that was patented by Stuart W. Cramer in 1906— a system of fresh-air shafts and fans to provide ventilation for an entire building. The danger of wide open windows and the incalculability of breezes at a height of over 300 feet soon became evident in the high-rises—just as industrial smog was becoming a problem at the street level.

Antonio Gaudí

From a historical point of view, Antonio Gaudí y Cornet (1852–1926), born in the Catalan region of north-ern Spain, is undoubtedly the single most influential Spanish architect, and a visionary pioneer of expressionist architecture (see page 148). When the young architect presented his first project in 1878, a plan for the Casa Vicens in Barcelona, observers could scarcely believe their eyes as they gazed at an apparently nightmarish mixture of Moorish and Gothic elements whose curved facade was not only covered with soft rounded forms, but at times leaned backwards, and at times leaned forward into space— a design that apparently emanated from Gaudí's initial training in the metal-working industry. As if that were not enough, the building seemingly sprouted a mushroom-formed roof and numerous small towers, the whole was painted a glaring yellow, and the ground plan consisted of an incomprehensible labyrinth (147).

[146] Daniel Hudson Burnham, the Fuller Flatiron Building, New York, 1902. Colored black-and-white photograph, ca. 1915.

[147] Antonio Gaudí: Casa Milà, Barcelona (1905–1910), ground plan. The completely asymmetrical rooms with their crooked and curved walls are grouped around courtyards and set back from one another on various levels. They are reached by a labyrinth of stairways and ramps.

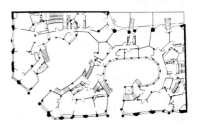

The New Path: Antonio Gaudí

[148] Antonio Gaudí: Casa Batló, Barcelona (1905–1907). A fine example of Gaudí's work, decorated with colored tiles and sculpturally ornamented with a rounded roof, bulging balcony railing, and small tower.

[149] Antonio Gaudí: Sagrada Familia cathedral, Barcelona (begun 1883; still under construction).

In an age of academic historicism, an irrationalism that deviated from the ennobling historical designs came as a shock. The amazement soon became a much-discussed and controversial sensation as Gaudí not only continued to propose more buildings in this striking style (see illus. 147) in subsequent years, but—thanks to the patronage of the wealthy industrialist Count Güell—was also able to build them. In addition to a number of town houses, Gaudí's work included a mansion for Güell (built 1885–1889) as well as a park in Barcelona bearing his patron's name (1900). This work sent architectural criticism into a tailspin, and even today, bold and flexible terms are needed to do even partial justice to Gaudí's designs. In the words of the architectural historian Wolfgang Pehnt, "After the turn of the [19th] century, Gaudí drew the richly wild and imaginative inventions and compilations of his early work together into large sculptural masses.... The structures turned into lively and animistic images that appeared to strike out rebelliously according to their own laws, to hiccup, to sprout limbs and elements, to blow bubble-like forms out of themselves. The Casa Milà [148; built 1905–1910] is a rock containing many cavities that seem to be washed over by the seaweed of the cast-iron balcony railings. Where the theory of the never-before-seen has the upper hand, being surprised by the absurd soon become the rule."

Architecture as a living, natural mass—this dream of architectural theorists, the proverbial "primitive cottage" (see illus. 39), appears to have been called into being at the hands of an architect entirely ignorant of such theory. Gaudí's buildings force one to think of designed caves, of sculpturally formed mounds, of inhabitable plants—in short, of a remarkably realistic fairy realm. The building materials and colors of his structures underline this impression of extraordinary closeness to nature, and yet at the same time the forms are often countered with sharp metallic ridges and points. With his work, Gaudí started a trend still in effect today—a movement back to nature, to a natural and ecological architecture. The elements of Gaudí that still seemed to be fragmented and fragile have found their so to speak "politically correct" modern fulfillment in the work of the Austrian Friedensreich Hundertwasser (see page 148).

What is at once Gaudí's masterpiece and legacy is the cathedral *Sagrada Familia* ("Sacred Family") in Barcelona (149). Originally planned and even begun in the neo-Gothic style, the building was an unfinished torso when Gaudí took it over from the city administration in 1883. He then molded the whole into a massive sculpture reaching toward the heavens, a fantastical expressionist monument of gigantic dimensions. The building functioned as a kind of open field for his architectural imagination, and he remained involved with it throughout the entire course of his career. Unfinished at the time of Gaudí's death in 1926, work on the cathedral continues today, still according to the architect's plans.

Gaudí's unique ideas and creations naturally attracted followers, especially in his native Spain. As his style slowly began to be accepted, and later jubilantly celebrated, by the Spanish establishment, numerous architects took up the formal language of the master. Gaudí's

[150] Josep Maria Jujol: Torre de la Creu, Sant Joan Despi (built 1913–1916). A school of Catalan expressionism based on Gaudí's understanding of architecture developed even during Gaudí's lifetime.

Form follows function." This central slogan of modern architecture, attributed to the American architect Louis Sullivan (1856–1924), is most clearly and consistently seen in industrial architecture. The mechanization of the old factories and the beginning of mass production in the early 20th century lent increasing emphasis to the premises in which the new processes were carried out. Industrial architecture not only demonstrated modernity in the areas of building technology and design, but also served as an outstanding medium of display, creating a show piece ideally suited to the immediate visualization of the economic and social ambitions of the factory owner or firm. The technical revolution of the 19th century, with its intelligently designed buildings of brick, iron and glass (see page 125 sq.), had paved the way for the universally malleable and pragmatic structures required by the age.

Another crucial factor that influenced the external form of industrial buildings of the 19th and early 20th century was the need for adequate lighting. One important aim of architectural design was to erect large factory halls with a flexible interior suitable to production, and at the same time to provide them with as much daylight as possible. Especially in the years before it became common to use electric lighting, good natural lighting was a very important factor in optimizing productivity. This need led to the construction of filigree architectonic shells—either buildings with huge windowed facades of glazed iron beams, or brick buildings that strained the limits of structural engineering by literally dissolving into innumerable small windows. One example is the wool factory constructed in 1909/1910 in Augsburg, Germany, colloquially known as the "glass palace."

Value was placed not just on these utilitarian concerns, however, but also on a decorative exterior. Often 19th century factory buildings were fitted out in a style that approached that of public buildings of state. Because factories in that age were usually located on the private property of the owners, and often close to their own residences (for example, the Villa Hügel near the Krupp works in Essen, Germany), the factories became a component in the self-aggrandizement of a class of newly rich industrialists who oriented themselves on aristocratic ideals.

In addition to these basic aspects, 20th century industrial architecture tends, in a particular way, to be the focus of pioneering architectural work—industrial buildings are a commercial, image-building medium. The

Industrial Architecture: A New Task for Architecture

[151] Peter Behrens: Turbine hall of the AEG factory in Berlin-Wedding. Main facade with AEG signet in the "pediment."

image becomes even more important as single factories increasingly grow into large "concerns," that is, impersonal and abstract corporations with stockholders, ever further removed from the once-close relationship between private owners and their factories.

A well-known example of this phenomenon is the turbine hall of the AEG electrical firm (built 1908/1909; 151) in a district of Berlin, designed by Peter Behrens, one of the most important German expressionist architects (see page 148). The engineering framework of the structure, with its front of high windows that flood the interior with light, is unashamedly obvious to the viewer, but the visible structure takes on artistic overtones in its resemblance to ancient temples

supported by columns. In the same sense, the artfully designed AEG signet on the "pediment" of the building becomes a focal point of the exterior design, replacing the sculptured gods and heroes on the gable ends of ancient temples. A classicist arrangement bounded by tin-capped masonry, Behrens' building contrasts with the older AEG building in that it consciously displays the desired image of modernity without forsaking references to historical building models and the architecture of display.

Another milestone of modern industrial architecture is the Fagus Shoe Factory, erected 1910–1914 in Alsfeld-an-der-Leine in Germany (152). The architects were Adolf Meyer and the young Walter

[152] Walter Gropius and Adolf Meyer: Administration building of the Fagus factory in Alsfeld-an-der-Leine.

Gropius. The administration building they designed, a long, three-storied rectangular cube with a carefully thought-out glass-steel facade containing stories and staircases that appear to be hanging from invisible points, became a hotly discussed building at the exhibition of the Cologne Werkbund of 1914, and established Gropius' reputation as a pioneer of the modern (see page 144 sq.).

An especially active and devoted patron of contemporary architecture was and is the Italian firm of Olivetti. Planned in the 1930s in the rationalist style of "fascist modern" (see page 150/51), the factory complex at Ivrea near Milan was only partially completed at that time, but later became an ideal example of modern-day architecture. Olivetti was also heavily involved in the continuation of *razionalismo* in the period after World War II. The completion of the works at Ivrea, and in particular the construction of a factory for telecommunications equipment built in Pozzuoli, Italy by Luigi Cosenzain (1951–1953; 153), are unarguable milestones in Italian architectural history, and have provided models for numerous other industrial projects. With its light-flooded buildings scattered throughout the grounds and numerous connecting passages supported on columns and set on several levels, the Pozzuoli complex—erected on a site already used in ancient times—drew inspiration from an old Roman villa built by the emperor Hadrian in the 2nd century AD in the vicinity of Rome at Tivoli.

Today, buildings for industry, trade, and services constitute first-class prestige objects, functioning in a sense as the billboards of the firm. Modern architectural design also plays an important role in imparting a firm's philosophy, and is therefore the object of sometimes considerable expenditure, as can be seen in the administration building of the Siemens firm in Munich (154). In this case, the form can only in a limited sense

[153] Luigi Cosenza: View of the "atrium" in the main building of the Olivetti factory in Pozzuoli. Photograph from 1955.

be said to follow technically related function. Rather, the need to make an impressive visible statement of the "corporate identity" of the firm is the true motivating force behind the design.

[154] Siemens office building, St.-Martinstrasse, Munich (built 1992). Design by Siemens building division. The complex, which was conceived as an open, multi-purpose office city, conveys simultaneously a sense of modernity and trusted tradition.

[155] Victor Horta: hallway of the van Eetvelde House, Brussels, built 1897–1900. An Art Nouveau interior.

erstwhile co-worker, Josep Maria Jujol (150) became his most important representative and successor.

Adolf Loos and Art Nouveau architecture

Art Nouveau—literally "new art," also known as the *Jugendstil* (German), *stile liberty* (Italian), or simply as the modern style to its contemporaries—constituted a comprehensive revolution in every facet of decoration and design. The Art Nouveau movement arose in several places simultaneously in reponse to the excessive and rigid application of historical models by the historicism of the late 19th century, becoming the first coherent style to radically rejected them. The leading hallmarks of the new approach were vegetative forms, curved lines, and a sense of movement conveyed in figural or abstract ornaments. The style was initially limited to graphic design, painting, furniture-making, textile art, porcelain, and metal objects, but around 1890 a specific architecture arose that was not only heavily decorated with applied ornamentation in the Art Nouveau tradition, but also raised plastic forms and extreme colorfulness into new stylistic principles. Perhaps the most famous example of this playfully ornamental architecture so rich in colors and forms remains the entryway for the Paris Metro stations, designed by Hector Guimard, that opened in 1900. (The filigree iron

[156] Charles Rennie Mackintosh: "Country house for an artist," 1901. Prepared almost in the style of graphic art, the design for this (unbuilt) house shows Mackintosh's vision of an Art Nouveau structure. Water-colored lead and pen drawing, Mackintosh Collection, University of Glasgow.

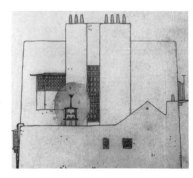

and glass work have been recently restored.) The universal nature of *Art Nouveau* was particularly strong in interior architectural design. The standard bearers in this regard are the Belgian Victor Horta (155), and later his fellow countryman Henry van der Velde. The Scottish architect Charles Rennie Mackintosh (156) also achieved a smelting of *Art Nouveau* principles and architecture, impressively apparent in his design for the School of Art in Glasgow, founded in 1896.

[157] Otto Wagner: Majolika House, Vienna. Photograph of the just-completed house (1899). The roof ridge iron railings, and in particular the colored glazed decoration—but not the abstract cubic body of the building—are reminiscent of *Art Nouveau*.

The overflowing richness of ornamentation and increasing formal excesses of *Art Nouveau* were meanwhile leading to a countermovement, whose epicenter was found in Vienna. Here Otto Wagner (1841–1918), and later some of his students such as Joseph Maria Olbrich and Josef Hoffmann, attempted to create a "moderate" Art Nouveau. Wagner returned to simple cubic forms (157) whose ornamentation was clearly rooted in *Art Nouveau*, but in combination with abstract exteriors that evaded the modish contemporary forms. Wagner's treatise on modern architecture, published in 1895, attempted to legitimate these developments theoretically and present them as timelessly valid. Indeed, they stood in sharp contrast to the expressionistic architecture that was rooted in "traditional" *Art Nouveau*.

This countermovement, known as the *Vienna Secession*, provided the foundation for the extremely radical ideas and concepts of the Moravian-born architect Adolf Loos (1870–1933), chiefly active in Austria. Loos's designs can best be understood as marking the true end of the *Art Nouveau* tradition and providing a transition into the classic modern age. His polemic essays, first published in various newspapers and magazines and later in book form (his treatise *Ornament and Crime* brought him fame) unmercifully attacked as a basic evil of the modern world not only the tendency to exuberant decoration, but also and in particular every form of architecture still based on the past. His buildings, however, including various town houses in Vienna and

Prague, are not at all Spartan in design. Their interiors are dominated by a sophisticated luxury; and the exteriors, although characterized by clear contours and the rational organization of the facades, by no means renounce elements designed to impress the observer. Loos' combination apartment and business building, Goldmann & Salatsch on the Michaelerplatz in Vienna(158), rises in the form of a simple white cubic structure above an unusually high ground floor, and is clad in magnificent marble.

[158]   Adolf Loos: apartment and commercial building Goldmann & Salatsch, Michaelerplatz, Vienna, built 1909–1911.

Bauhaus architecture

Today *Bauhaus* is a synonym for the architecture and lifestyle of what has come to be known as classical modern, a movement arising between the wars in the German Weimar Republic. Characterized by artistic and intellectual innovation, the resulting architecture displays clear lines, a marked preference for cubes and rectangles, a construct principle based on the linking of cube-shaped building and design elements, and interiors revealing completely functional design. (Nothing illustrates this image more clearly than the British rock group that consciously adopted the name "*Bauhaus*" in the early 1980s to illustrate the modernity of their abstract music.) In the strikingly contoured shapes of industrial products, the classical modern direction of the *Bauhaus* school of the late 1920s took aim against the flourishes and adornments of the late Art Nouveau and expressionism. In this sense, the term "*Bauhaus*," like the term "*Art Nouveau*," implies far more than an architectural style: It signifies a comprehensive idea of contemporary modern design.

The term "*Bauhaus*" is closely linked with the name of its inventor and founder, Walter Gropius (1883–1969), who had succeeded Henry van der Velde in 1919 as the director of the School of Applied Arts in Weimar. Gropius's perception of the close connection between architecture and the other areas of crafts and design led him to give up his initial intention to emphasize architecture, and in the end he allowed his "new" *Bauhaus* to retain the "old" character of a universal school of the applied arts. When the environment in Weimar proved unsupportive of the academy, it resettled in Dessau in 1925 in a move that offered welcome possibilities for breaking with tradition. The artistic faculty assembled under Gropius in the new location reads as a "Who's Who" of modernism: Paul Klee, Wassily Kandinsky, Marcel Breuer, Johannes Itten, Josef Albers, Lionel Feininger, and other prominent fine and applied artists had their studios and workshops in Dessau.

[159] Walter Gropius: *Bauhaus*, Dessau (built 1925/1926).

The new, comprehensive *Bauhaus* idea—which at its core involved a complete reorientation of architecture and design to contemporary needs, and thus constituted an equally complete rejection of formal borrowings from historical modes—did not spring into existence from a momentary inspiration of Gropius, but had important predecessors. One of these was the German *Werkbund* movement, which advocated the intelligent design and production of mass goods for the

The New Path: Bauhaus Architecture

[160] Gerrit Thomas Rietveld: Schröder House, Utrecht, Holland (built 1924). The living and dining rooms are on the second floor. Photograph from 1995.

general populace. Formed around an exhibition in 1914, the group soon fell asunder in unbreachable disagreements over such issues as artistic creativity versus the need to standardize design for the masses. In reaction to the English Arts and Crafts movement, the Werkbund formulated its vision of architecture primarily in industrial terms. In addition to Peter Behrens and Hans Poelzig, Walter Gropius himself, who had once worked for Behrens, was an enthusiastic supporter of this school of architecture in his younger years.

The *Bauhaus* also owed a large debt of gratitude to the Dutch group of architects known as *De Stijl*, named after a journal of design and initiated by Theo van Doesburg (1883–1931). As was later the case in the *Bauhaus*, in *De Stijl* architecture, design and the fine arts were melded together into a single process. In the early days, the most important exponent of the movement was the painter Piet Mondrian. The maxim of the group was abstraction, which was related to the Spanish-French cubism of Pablo Picasso. *De Stijl's* claim to validity in both the crafts and architecture and its immense importance for the Bauhaus were embodied in Gerrit Thomas Rietveld (1888–1964), who had been trained as a master carpenter and furniture designer, and who became famous for his "red-blue chair" (1923; today in the Museum of Modern Art in New York). His innovative design for the Schröder House (160) built in Utrecht in 1924, with its rationally intersecting mobile-like rectangular surfaces, its outer shell with a variable window-wall structure, and its offset stories in the interior, which are invisibly attached and thus give the impression of floating in air, became an incentive for *Bauhaus* architecture and an example of the classical modern.

The new building complex of the art academy at Dessau (159), designed by Gropius and built largely according to his plans within two years (1925/1926), became the touchstone of *Bauhaus* architecture. Buildings that housed workshops, cafeterias, and student dormitories held to

strict *Bauhaus* principles. In particular, the "artists' housing," which provided living quarters for the faculty, still stand today as masterpieces of Bauhaus architecture in both their interior and exterior design. Neither, however, is conceivable without Rietveld's Schröder House. Various new housing developments built according to *Bauhaus* standards (the Weissenhof development near Stuttgart or the Kalkerfeld settlement by Cologne, for example) made good the Bauhaus claim of effective design for the masses and still lent eloquent expression to the Bauhaus as the ultimate modern architecture (161).

[161] Le Corbusier (1887–1965) and Pierre Jannaret: Duplex 14/15 in the Weissenhof housing development near Stuttgart, built in 1927. From a 1929 advertisement of the Mercedes-Benz company: "Here the idea of the connection between automobile and architecture goes a long way to support Corbusier's understanding of [architecture as a] 'machine for living'."

With Gropius' resignation in 1928 and the appointment of his chosen follower, the architect Ludwig Meyer, as director of the *Bauhaus*, the internal balance of the institution shifted in the direction of architecture. When Meyer was removed for political reason two years later, his successor, the

[162] Ludwig Mies van der Rohe: German pavilion for the 1929 World's Fair at Barcelona. Photograph from 1991.

architect Ludwig Mies van der Rohe (1886–1969), increased this emphasis in ways that are still visible today. His pavilion for the 1929 World's Fair in Barcelona (162) demonstrates the advance of *Bauhaus* ideas in its ever increasing abstraction, the dissolution of all materially dominated

tectonics, the reduction of the structure to a minimum required by engineering requirements, and the interplay of interior and exterior.

The Bauhaus at Dessau closed under pressure from the radical fascist right wing in 1932; its protagonists Gropius and Mies van der Rohe emigrated, but not before unsuccessfully submitting entries in contests for prominent Nazi architectural projects (such as the Reichsbank building in Berlin). In the United States, Bauhaus ideas found a welcome reception, and were adjusted to suit the altered needs. Both Gropius and Mies van der Rohe became much sought-after and highly respected architects in the United States; in particular, the business district of Chicago underwent major renovations under the Bauhaus influence. Furthermore, the ever-changing architecture of an individualist like Frank Lloyd Wright (1869–1959) would be unimaginable without the influence of Bauhaus.

Expressionism: Rudolf Steiner's Goetheanum and the architecture of Friedensreich Hundertwasser

In his ground-breaking monograph *Expressionist Architecture* (1973), the architectural historian Wolfgang Pehnt identified a category of modern architecture defined by a kind of expressionistic, sculpture-like design. The strong and expressive design of these buildings tends to reject tectonic principles and instead reveal their origin—i.e., the

[163] Rudolf Steiner's Goetheanum in Dornach, Switzerland, 1924–1928: View of the south-western side at dusk.

identity of the builder—by means of their striking aesthetic, political, religious, and social content. The basic idea for this kind of architecture goes back to the *architecture parlante* ("speaking architecture") of 17th and 18th century French theorists, who developed a concept of "semantic" building design (see page 114). In the early 20th century, Antonio Gaudí was another important exponent of this approach (see page 135).

Rudolf Steiner is the controversial founder of anthroposophy, a philosophical approach that emphasizes the intuitive powers of human beings and the role of the arts in developing them. Steiner turned to an expressionist mode in 1923 in order to rebuild the Goetheanum, the headquarters of the anthroposophical movement near Basel, Switzerland, after the first structure was lost to fire. Based on Steiner's models, a domed, cathedral-like building was erected (completed in 1928) using smooth concrete to produce an exaggerated formal "language" (163, 164). The building's innovative rejection of right angles (with the exception of several door and window apertures) became the model for much subsequent anthroposophist architecture. Steiner's design also incorporates a dramatic use of light. The plasticity of the building's monotone gray concrete exterior allows a fascinating play of light and shadow, just as the large, at times Tiffany-style, windows lend a vitalizing element to the harmonious impression created by the whole. Similarly, the windows provide an excitingly colorful contrast to the supposedly "cold" concrete. By means of expressionism, the building thus becomes an impressive embodiment of anthroposophy.

A later representative of this form of expression-ism is the contemporary Viennese architect and painter, Friedensreich Hundertwasser. In the decades since 1970, his buildings have made use not only of

[164] Rudolf Steiner's Goetheanum in Dornach, Switzerland, 1924–1928: View of the west staircase.

[165] Friedensreich Hundertwasser: Renovation of the train station in Uelzen, Germany. Model, 1999.

plastic forms (often in the name of ecology), but most strikingly, of color. The polychrome design, closely related to Hundertwasser's painting, causes the buildings to stand out strikingly in the midst of today's city landscapes, and has become a trademark. The architect takes particular interest in the expressionist renovation of existing buildings in need of repair. The unflourished flat colorfulness of the model he presented in 1999 for the renovation of the train station in Uelzen, Germany (165), originally dating from 1880, forms a charming contrast to the brick Wilhelmine building with its applied classicist ornamentation.

The perversion of the modern: Architectural totalitarianism under Mussolini, Hitler, and Stalin

"Architecture and Power in Europe under the Dictators" was the effective title of an exhibition that made its way through various large European cities in 1996. In the 20th century, architecture demonstrated that it could be of particular service as a medium for display and ideological formulas—in short, as a manifestation of dominance and the glorification of power in modern totalitarian systems—and that it was capable of unscrupulously using the progressive modern style as well. The fusion of the modern with the totalitarian is equally clear in its use at times of a considerable variety of other architectural forms, historically-derived motives, and various intentions within the various European dictatorships of the 20th century.

Unlike the architecture of Nazi Germany, the architecture of fascist Italy has been for a considerable while a legitimate subject for serious aesthetic analysis. In Italy, a number of very different architectural styles developed from the modern movement, whose common denominator was to be found in their opposition to Antonio Sant'Elia and Mario Chiattone, whose supposedly "nihilistic" futurism radically rejected all that was traditional. Backward references to the architectural history of the nation, in particular to ancient Rome, became the prevailing theme of the fascists, expressing itself in a number of extremely different architectural forms. The *Scuola Romana* (leading exponent: Marcello Paicentini) pursued a modernized but monumental classicism, a prominent example of which is Enrico del Dobbio's Foro Mussolini in Rome, begun in 1927. On the other hand, the representatives of the *novocento* tendency made use of classical forms, but largely as minimalized ornamentation applied to an architecture otherwise based on the principles of the modern. The pictures of the painter Giorgio de Chirico (1888–1978) functioned here as structural inspiration. Razionalismo, pursued by the *Gruppo Sette* ("group of seven") and later the *Movimento per l'Architettura Razionale*, or MAR, developed the "white modern" trend: a contemporary, almost jewel-like architecture that at the same time reached back to classical antiquity for many of its design principles. The Casa del Fascio, the regional headquarters of the Fascist Party in Como erected by the pioneer of Italian rationalism, Giuseppe Terragni, between 1932 and 1936 is an example of this style.

Architects of all three of these stylistic directions sought to legitimize their positions theoretically in their writings, and they competed with each other vigorously. Not until the late 1930s were these "schools" melded into a kind of national style, in which the intellectually more challenging *Razionalismo* took the ascendancy. A further emphasis of fascist architecture was urban architectural concepts. Complete drawing-board cities, such

[166]   A sign of fascist modernity in the midst of a historical setting: the Casa del Fascio in Como, Italy, presents itself as an architectural jewel in its monumental Baroque environment. With its transparent glass-house architecture, it visualized the mutual control of the people and those in power. Aerial photograph from 1936.

[167] Scale models placed next to each other: the huge Great Hall of the People (designed by Albert Speer, 1939; 1,050 ft. from floor to top of dome with a foundation of 1,082 feet on each side) and the German Reichstag in Berlin (Paul Wallot, (built 1884–1894). The classicist Brandenburg Gate appears to be a very delicate work by comparison.

as Sabaudia, situated in the drained Pontine swamps south of Rome, became models of fascist architecture and social imagination.

In contrast to fascist Italy, neither pluralistic competition nor an intellectual foundation in the service of creating an "architecture of state" was a major concern of the National Socialist (Nazi) movement in Germany. Nazi architecture—which exists largely in the form of models and drawings rather than actual buildings due to the unforeseen brevity of the "1000-year Reich"—bears instead a more monarchic stamp, designed to impress observers through sheer size and splendor and to force them into submission. A statement by Hitler on the planned "Great Hall of the People" (167), with its immense domed chamber for 200,000 persons—quoted by his architectural minister Alfred Speer—illustrates these intentions clearly: "Let a small farmer step into our great domed hall: It will take his breath away. From then on, he will know his place."

Nazi architecture, with its massive stone-block construction, angular pilasters, columns crowned with capitals and sophisticatedly organized facades, is often seen as deriving its inspiration from the ancient classic age. In fact, however, the architecture is eclectic, reflecting extremely varied historical references, including Baroque, Renaissance, Romanesque, and early Christian church architectural influences. In those cases where a reference to antiquity is clear, it more often refers to a stage of classicism of the new age than to the Greco-Roman world. An example here is the final phase of the Munich Königsplatz designed by Paul Ludwig Troost shortly before his death in 1934 and completed in 1937. The pavilions on their pilasters (the "Temple of Honor") reveal themselves to be formally analogous to the 19th-century designs of Klenze, which dominated the plazas in which they were built. What appears to be "classical" is, in fact, not a reference to the ancient world, but to the new national-classicist architectural tradition of the 19th century.

On the surface, the architecture of the Stalinist period in the Soviet Union seems just as historically oriented as that of the other totalitarian states. Focused not on the classical Mediterranean world, but rather on the czarist-Orthodox models dating from before the Bolshevik revolution, the architecture is therefore national in character to the highest degree—a curious contradiction of an internationally oriented ideology with internationally leading representatives of an avant-garde in the fine arts and architecture such as El Lissitzky. In this self-proclaimed most advanced of all societies, surprisingly, the modern plays almost no role at all. The "imperial style for proletarians" instead used various ennobling models drawn from the ancient classic world, the Renaissance, and the Baroque (for example, the theater of the Red Army in Moscow, built 1935–1940; the Moscow subway stations). In the post-war period Soviet architecture emphasized—and exported to the Warsaw Pact members—an ornamental "sugar-coated" style (Moscow State University, Moscow, built 1948–1952), whose gigantic flourishes oriented on czarist decoration simultaneously attempted to demonstrate originality and assure a collective national identity (168).

[168] An example of Stalinist "sugar-coated" modern style.
Moscow State University in Moscow, built in 1948.

In almost all societies, architecture serves as one of the most durable and therefore powerfully effective cultural media. Even the ruins of centuries-old buildings bear witness to their former appearance, purpose, and significance. Furthermore, many historic buildings remain in service for generations, often even up to present times. Nonetheless, it is quickly forgotten that a parallel genre of architecture exists where this durability cannot be taken for granted—indeed, it is even planned from the beginning to be other-wise—temporary structures meant to be removed after a limited period of use. All ages have known such ephemeral projects. Information about such architecture naturally tends to be limited because of the fact that the structures do not sur-vive, but nonetheless offers enrich-ment to the architectural under-standing of various epochs.

Even in ancient times, various kinds of temporary buildings played an important architectural role. Numerous ceremonial and festival structures of the Greek-Hellenic kings (late 4th to 1st century BC) are mentioned in classical literature as noteworthy examples of royal splendor. Some were even described in very great detail, as for example the festival tent of Alexander the Great, the huge gilded wooden cere-monial ship of the Egyptian king Ptolemaios IV (truly a floating pal-ace), and above all the festival tent of Ptolemaios II, richly decorated with gold, ivory, and priceless purple dye. Ancient Rome was also the site of many temporarily erected wooden structures, but the aim in this case was more pragmatic. Until well into the 1st century BC, it was customary to erect tribunals for dramas and gladiator contests—and then to dismantle them immediately after the show, because the gathering of adrenaline-filled, fanatically excited crowds carried too high a risk factor in the eyes of the Roman Senate.

In addition to the building and dismantling of tribunal structures—a phenomenon found in almost all phases of architectural history, such as in the knightly tournaments of medieval Europe—temporary archi-tecture also includes the ephemeral tents made by nomad tribes and other shelters derived directly from natural surroundings (see page 34). Since the 16th century, however, the theater backdrop has been the pri-mary venue for temporary architec-tural structures and creating the illusion of buildings. So-called "Po-temkin villages"—now legendary—are an early example of this pheno-menon: backdrops of house facades with which Prince Grigory Potemkin deceived the Russian Empress Catherine the Great as to the true social condition of her empire. Centuries later, the numerous wooden stage sets produced at the behest of Albert Speers, Hitler's architectural minister, were built as

[169] Scene from *Metropolis* by Fritz Lang (1929). This film's architecture proved to be formative for many decades.

full-scale models for future Nazi projects, but were never transformed into reality.

The use of architectural scenery is especially important in theater and film—and is often amazingly successful. Today's popular conception of an American small "wild west" town is only a fictional cliché, arising from the stereotyped sets used in Hollywood films of the 1940s and 1950s. Several decades later, sophisticated video processes brought illusionary techniques to the service of film architecture, as in the 1982 film *Blade Runner*. Such structures, however, are never pure inventions, but rather mixtures of alienated versions of buildings drawn from real architectural history and science fiction visions. According to the film architect Lawrence G. Paull, he combined photographs of arcades and facade elements from Milan, Italy with motifs drawn from Egyptian art, along with more modern ideas stemming from art deco, Gaudí, or Frank Lloyd Wright. His aim? A city of the year 2020 where Conan the Barbarian might feel at home.

Since the 1930s, another important application for temporary architecture has been the booths and stands at trade fairs—usually a show piece used only once, but nonetheless a mixture of stage setting and "real" architecture. Similar to a stage or film set, these fair booths can be extremely imaginative, but at the same time must function as real structures in that they have an interior that can be entered and support activities that take place inside the "set." The conception and design of such booths today constitutes a carefully thought-out and closely calculated task for specialists. As with the design of industrial structures (see page 138), trade booths must also create a convincing setting for the special character of a competitive product or relay a firm's identity—with references to historical traditions as well as recourse to contemporary, ultra-modern concepts of space and form (170).

[170] The trade fair booth as an open, multi-storied house: The highly regarded VebaCOM stand at the Cebit computer fair in Hanover, Germany, 1996.

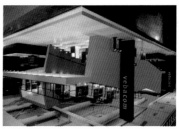

The triumph of modernity? Between brutalism and high tech

In the decades following 1945, "global architecture" has taken on so many different forms that it is almost impossible to provide a balanced and comprehensive overview. However, whether concentrated in one local-ity or found throughout the globe, the common deno-minator of all the various trends lies in the classical modern style and its forerunners. The architecture of the period between 1910 and 1930 clearly provided the foundation for almost all the developments of design and construction that emerged in the second half of the 20th century (with the striking exception of post-modernism). In other words, with very few exceptions, present-day architecture has recycled and elaborated upon its historical models, but not outgrown them.

Clearly rooted in the classical modern is the pheno-menon generally known by the catchword "brutalism" (derived from the French term *beton brut*, or "raw con-crete"). The term was initially coined by the British team of Alison and Peter Smithson to designate a particularly puritanical building concept characterized by absolute truth to material, complete visibility of all building materials, and a total rejection of plaster or facings. In today's usage, the term goes even further to include characteristics that allow brutalism to be seen as a perversion of both the formal and social content of the classical modern; brutalism in fact implies an in-creasingly inhuman concept of living and urban con-struction. Le Corbusier's "machines for living"—gigan-tic high-rise complexes possessing an almost complete urban infrastructure—included units for habitation, work, and the provision of supplies. In the ideal case, the inhabitants of these "machines" would never need to leave the premises (171). Such "machines" are, at least theoretically, the forerunners of the dismal, ghetto-like concrete complexes that were initially celebrated in the 1950s as an architectural and social ideal (see illus. 175). In the United States such buildings are often found at the heart of decaying inner city areas, whereas

[171] The prototypical "machine for living": Le Corbusier's *Unité d'Habitation* in Marseilles, built 1945–1951. A similar building, incorporating roof gardens, shops, offices, and apartments of widely varying layouts and sizes (some stretching over three stories), was constructed in the 1950s near the Olympic Stadium in Berlin.

in Europe and the Third World they appear as satellite towns on the outskirts of metropolitan areas. In any case, the concept soon proved itself to be a fatal mistake.

In essence, plasticism—an imaginative sculptural style using the universally malleable raw material of concrete—is related to brutalism in its truth-of-material, but plasticism's rejection of a rationalist approach has allowed it to emerge as a radically different architectural principle whose roots are to be sought in the expressionism of the 1920s (see page 148). High points of this architectural style, which had a decisive influence on the 1950s, are Le Corbusier's pilgrimage chapel Notre-Dame-du-Haut in Ronchamps, France, and Frank Lloyd Wright's Guggenheim Museum in New York (172).

Born in the 1960s and remaining a pampered child of architecture to this day is the futuristic-looking high tech style, which in a sense constitutes a continuation of 19th-century glass-and-iron buildings through modern techniques (see page 125). By means of its pipe-and-scaffold constructions, its suspended, multiple staggered story levels,

1964–1973
Vietnam War ends with costly American defeat in Indochina
1967
Six Day War between Israel and Egypt
1968
Change of power in Czechoslovakia, "Prague Spring" suppressed by Soviet troops; student unrest in Germany and France
1978/79
Fundamentalist Islamic revolution in Iran
1989
Fall of the Berlin Wall; Soviet empire begins to crumble
1990–1991
Second Gulf War: UN alliance against Iraq after invasion of Kuwait, leading to economic collapse (1992–1999)
1999
NATO troops in Kosovo

[172] The Guggenheim Museum in New York, built by Frank Lloyd Wright (1956–1959). Ramps and spirals as "primal American" architectural elements (often seen in drive-in restaurants and parking garages) work together to form a spectacularly expressionist structure—despite its limited usefulness for the business of running the museum as such.

[173] The Pompidou Center in Paris, one of the exemplary works of modern high tech architecture. Renzo Piano and Richard Rogers, architects.

and its extremely interrupted or "broken" exterior facades, high tech offers an idealized vision of modernity—in short, it is architecture as the expression of the communication society. Famous examples of high tech include the Olympic Stadium in Munich (built 1968–1971; Günther Behnish and Partners, architects; see illus. 181), and most notably the Pompidou Center in Paris (built 1971–1977; 173). That this style more than any other continues to be seen as the flagship of modernity is clear from later examples. The Lloyds Building (built 1979–1984; Richard Rogers, architect) serves as an unmistakable eye-catcher in London's architecturally rather monotonous Bank District, and further high tech buildings stretch along the Thames dock area, renovated in the 1980s. A prime example on the East India Dock is the printing building of the Financial Times, designed by Nicholas Grimshaw in 1986–1988. Sir Norman Foster's renovation of the German Reichstag in Berlin, completed in 1999, also falls into the category of high tech architecture.

Although to some extent a fleeting architectural phenomenon of the 1990s, deconstructivism is perhaps the most original concept of the first half of the 20th century. This does not mean that it lacks historical models, however, being related to the Russian constructivist movement of the 1920s, as the term "deconstruction," coined by Philip Johnson within the framework of an exhibit in 1988, implies. The hallmark of deconstructivism is "disturbed perfection"—the surprising break with the expected. Here, the *Bauhaus* motto "form follows function" finds itself transformed into a cheerfully care-free "form follows fantasy" (Bernhard Tschumi). At times, the resulting structures appear as if a childish giant had put together odd-looking combinations of building blocks. In addition to Bernhard Tschumi and the firm "COOP Himmelblau" (Co-op Sky-blue), the American architect Frank O. Gehry is particularly

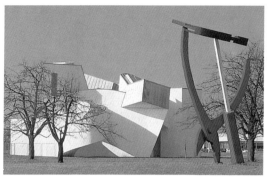

[174] A masterpiece of deconstructivism: The Vitra Design Museum near Basel (Frank O. Gehry, 1987–1989).

recognized as a protagonist of deconstructivism. Gehry's Vitra Design Museum, built 1987–1989 near Basel, Switzerland (174), and his Guggenheim Museum in Bilbao, Spain, are milestones of this architectural direction.

In addition to these major trends, there are numerous other architects and tendencies that are difficult to pigeonhole into categories of design and style. The American Richard Meier is one such "wanderer between worlds." His highly distinctive *œuvre*, exemplified in the new J.P. Getty Center in Santa Monica, California (1998), falls into the gap between various styles, paying obeisance to unornamented minimalism in the tradition of Adolf Loos, structuralism in the tradition of the Dutch *De Styjl* movement (and its present-day extension, the "white modern" of the Italian *Razionalismo*), as well as to classicist postmodernism.

A romanticized high tech style can be seen in the high-rises of German-born architect Helmut Jahn. Also falling outside the defined categories is a modern kind of functionalism—architecture that fulfills its purpose but simultaneously reveals its modern construction in its appearance. One of the protagonists of this direction is the German firm of Gerkan, Mang & Partners (Leipzig Fair Building; expansion of the Hamburg Airport). Fritz Leonhardt, pioneer of pre-stressed concrete work, has also played a leading role in the technical aspect of architecture. His bridge and tower designs have repeatedly caused furor since the 1940s (the highway bridge at Cologne-Rodenkirchen, Germany, 1941; Stuttgart

[175] Extreme poverty in the Third World: Slums near Bombay, India. Photograph, 1999.

television tower, 1954). A primary example of an imaginative use of high tech principles in the United States can be seen in the geodosic dome developed by R. Buckminster, found today throughout the world.

Slabs and corrugated metal: The dark side of "modern" life

Since the mid-20th century, the population of the world's large metropolitan centers has literally exploded. Migration from the countryside into cities and the failure of all-too-common and desperate attempts to make a living in the metropolitan areas have made urban centers, especially in the Third World, into fertile ground for social problems. Today, nearly 20 million people fill the cities of Lagos, Bombay, and Mexico City, with hardly fewer in Cairo and Rio de Janeiro.

This uncontrolled growth has not left architecture unscathed; indeed, a totally new category has arisen on the heels of this dramatic social development—an architecture whose driving forces are need and abject poverty, however odd it seems to include such motives as factors in architectural history. Here the focus is not on architecture as a sublime art, but in its most elementary form—architecture as protective shelter. This "lowly" architecture bears striking witness to the social realities of the second half of the 20th century. The quest for a roof over one's head has led to the growth of huge slums in and around the hopelessly overpopulated cities. New and unplanned urban districts—built on largely unsuitable terrain, without the least infrastructure of streets, sewage, electricity, or water—have sprung up as if in a fast-motion film. The most primitive structures are scarcely more than a thrown-together protection from rain and cold. All too often, the sole building policy of urban authorities is to tear down such slums and drive their inhabitants away, or to enclose them inside high walls in order to prevent them from damaging the city's image. Anyone who has visited Rio de Janeiro is aware of the horrifying contrast between the elegant life on the beaches of Copacabana and the misery of the ghetto that immediately borders it, but it is evident only on close inspection.

Within the slums, extreme poverty reigns—but this destitution in no way guarantees equality among the inhabitants, and the nature of their housing is essential proof of the social position of individual families. Those who can point to a corrugated metal hut of their own unquestionably belong to the "prosperous" class— a fortunate minority in possession of a comparatively sound building, often including modest "comforts" such as several rooms, a rain-proof roof, closable windows, and even some furniture. Further down the scale, inhabitants of flimsily constructed wooden huts decked with old and often torn plastic sheeting are considerably worse off— and yet still better off than the truly homeless who spend their nights on the street with nothing more than a blanket (175).

[176] Decayed residential area in Liverpool, England. Photograph, 1992.

[177]   Built in the former East Germany as a symbol of modernity, the satellite town of Berlin-Marzahn is a slab construction settlement for more than 20,000 inhabitants.

The slums of the developed nations differ from those of the Third World only by degree. Entire districts of large cities have decayed into slums in the past 40 years due to social erosion and repeated bouts of mass unemployment caused by breakdowns in industrial societies. In the United States and England, the "losers" face particularly drastic forms of exclusion. Large areas of apartment buildings that had been erected as speculative enterprises have become centers of poverty in which alternative, and often criminal, economic systems have developed—along with the new hierarchies associated with them. Under such circumstances, a slum can arise within a short time. The continuing arrival of new inhabitants, the development of social problem groups in districts with cheap housing, and the resulting departure of the "old inhabitants" are self-perpetuating and increasingly dynamic processes.

The boundary between socially subsidized apartments and a slum can be hazy. Many high-rise "projects" built for welfare families in the United States from the 1960s offer evidence of this. In Europe, the much-celebrated apartment projects erected in East Berlin in a rational, but hardly durable, slab construction as a modern solution to the housing problems of the 1970s and 1980s have proved not to be only a perversion of the modern idea in architecture, but also social dynamite. Such projects increasingly become the state-subsidized housing for fringe groups—architectonic symbols of violence, poverty, and hopelessness. The decay of such high-rise apartment buildings can only be prevented by great expenditures of money, which governments are often not willing to invest. In rare instances, as in New York city, project dwellers—often led by mothers fearful for their children's safety in the violent drug-ridden environment—have formed cooperative enterprises to "buy" the buildings from the government for a nominal sum in order to manage them communally for the good of the inhabitants.

Urban Transformations: New uses for old buildings

At first glance, the renovation and recycling of older buildings appears to be a phenomenon of the present age, an ecologically and historically motivated treatment of architecture. These new and positive values are radically different from the rule of the razing ball and the social damage inflicted by the concrete brutalism that dominated into the late 1970s. But the principle of adapting surviving architectural elements to fit entirely different needs is by no means entirely new. This process occurs in almost all cultures and all ages, and the variety of motives that lie behind it can be seen especially clearly by examining the large Italian cities with their thickly layered masses of historical building material.

[178] The Marcellus Theater in Rome, built in the 1st century AD, has provided living space continuously from the Middle Ages to the present.

As the buildings dating from the classical age of Rome decayed and collapsed through the centuries, the ruins were used for many different purposes. Often serving as quarries, they became a source of new buildings. In addition, it was not uncommon to recycle the huge remains of ancient public buildings, whose hulls were renovated and made inhabitable. From the 12th century, the Colosseum, the largest amphitheater of the ancient world, drew increasing numbers of inhabitants. Discrete apartments came into existence in various stories and passageways, reachable via a labyrinth of newly built stairways. Removed from the Colosseum by 19th-century architects, one can envision this housing by comparing it with the Marcellus Theater, conveniently located in the center of Rome near the Piazza Campo dei Fiori. The entire upper story of the ruins contains apartments (178), with shops and artisan workshops below. To take a later example, even the once proudly defiant city walls of Naples, dating from the 15th century, were transformed into living quarters in the 19th century.

In all these cases, a seemingly curious re-application of ancient historical structures occurred in response to a pressing need for more living space. Today, in stark contrast to these examples, the renovation of old structures into private living quarters often represents a phenomenon of luxury. At great expense and with much attention to detail, urban apartments are carved out of historical remains, and even combined into larger "apartment units": formerly crumbling country houses are elegantly enlarged, or abandoned train stations and mills are cleverly transformed into housing. Such examples demonstrate the current trends and ambitions of a certain well-earning social class.

In another direction and with other intentions, larger public or industrial building complexes have been converted and assigned new tasks in the last decades as historical preservation measures have become internationally widespread. The concept of architectural preservation for the sake of new use has triumphed in the conversion of such complexes into museums, cultural and public centers, or

[179] The interior of the Gare d'Orsay, today a highly respected museum located directly on the Seine. Designed by Victor Laloux, the building was dedicated in 1900 on the occasion of the Paris World's Fair.

occasionally into charitable institutions—a transfer of the buildings into the public or social sphere that is usually politically uncontested. The Paris train station Gare d'Orsay is a well-known example of such a restoration and dedication. Built in 1897 but out of service since 1945, it is now an art museum (179). In the United States, various pragmatic applications have arisen, as in the spectacular restoration of Union Station in St. Louis, Missouri. Opened in 1894, the

Sport and Leisure Architecture

Already in ancient Roman times— according to the motto "bread and circus"— there was a wide architectural repetoire of structures built in the service of leisure and pleasure—thermal baths, arenas and theaters are among the primary forms. The present leisure culture has intensively adopted not only these types of buildings, but also their former character. Today's sport stadiums, for example, with their rows of seats ringing an oval form are "Roman,"

[180] Caesar's Palace, Las Vegas, U.S.

based on the Roman Colosseum (see illus. 22). The myriad baths and water parks that have been created since the 1980s also have a Roman flavor. Another "Roman" inspiration are numerous casino venues, the outrageous Caesar's Palace in Las Vegas (180) being without doubt the prime example.

By way of contrast, two other types of leisure architecture represent areas of contemporary experimentation that are not retrospectively oriented: theaters and museums. Ever since the Renaissance, the ancient open air theater has been roofed and increasingly determined by the technical demands of performances. One variation of "classical" theater construction is the cinema, actually a separate type of building since ca. 1910 (Kottbusser Tor movie theater in Berlin, built by Bruno Taut). In the United States in the 1920s, cinemas increasingly became over-decorated settings that framed the films shown in them. The noble, classicist, exclusive museums of the late 18th and 19th centuries—ground breaking was the British Museum in London, founded in 1753—were opened to wide segments of the population in the late 20th

century, giving both architects and builders an extremely visible task that demanded a functional interior while allowing great freedom of expression in the exterior design. There is no prominent architect of the modern, postmodern, and present who has not been involved in a controversial debate over plans for a museum.

[181] Olympic Stadium, Munich.

165

The Architect: Artist, Technician, or Organizer?

An animated debate arose in architectural circles in the fall of 1999 when Sir Norman Foster, who had been appointed the chief architect for the renovation of the German Reichstag building in Berlin, insisted on his right to forbid any architectural alterations, even the addition of furnishings, the hanging of pictures, or placement of potted plants. Once more the question of the role and the (self-)understanding of the archi-tect arose, and it again became clear that there is hardly a profession that has undergone greater changes in the course of the centuries than that of the architect.

In the high cultures of the Far East and ancient Egypt as well as those of the classical West, architects were by today's standards "amateurs"; most importantly, they were not artists. Possessed of technical skills, their chief task was the logistical organization of

[182] Sir Christopher Wren presents the English king Charles II his designs for the rebuilding of London; Copper engraving dating from ca. 1670.

what at times were highly complex building processes; meanwhile, all the details of design depended on the ideas of the project owner. Kings and pharaohs, the public assemblies of the Greek city states, the priests of the various shrines, the Roman Senate, later the Roman emperor, and the bishops of the Christian communities—all these parties, but not the architect, determined the form and design of the larger, non-private buildings.

Initially, the chosen or appointed architects stemmed from the citizenry or officialdom, figures who sometimes only functioned a single time in this role, like Libon, for example, the architect on record for the temple of Zeus on Olympia. Not until the Hellenistic age (beginning in the 3rd century BC) did a certain professionalization develop. It is therefore not surprising that, until the Middle Ages, works of architecture were

[183] Jacques Gabriel—a painted portrait of an architect, strikingly similar to the prototypical image of a French aristocrat of the 18th century.

linked with the names of those who commissioned them, and only in rare cases with the architect.

For the first time in history, the city states of the Italian Renaissance gave rise to the ideal of the freely creating architect whose designs derived from aesthetic considerations, and who was on the whole obedient only to his own genius. (As in the graphic arts during this period, the role of the architect was an indication of the new secular possibilities of architecture, which until then had been limited to religious contexts.) Giotto di Bondone, Brunelleschi, and Alberti were the first prominent figures of this new profession. They designed according to their own credos in the light of classical models; furthermore, the objects of their work were no longer determined solely by the clergy, but increasingly by secular rulers. Not without reason did Alberti dedicate his *Ten Books on Architecture* to the Florentine ruler Lorenzo di Medici in humbly formulated praise of the prince.

In this new climate, the architect was transformed into a sought-after specialist, with corresponding opportunities to rise in society. Few of the famous architects of the Renaissance died without having amassed a fortune, and often a title, to pass on to his heirs. In the 16th and 17th centuries, the prominent architects of the

[184]   The ruler as architect: Frederick II of Prussia, design for central section and side wings of the Prince Heinrich Palace in Berlin, ca. 1797.

The Architect: Artist, Technician, or Organizer?

Baroque were very well paid and highly honored members of the court, and their high ranking status was mirrored self-confidently in portraits: A copper engraving dating from around 1670, for example, depicts the British master architect Sir Christopher Wren as an elevated member of the court presenting his plans for the rebuilding of London after the great fire of 1666 to King Charles II (182).

A further improvement of the architectural profession occurred in France in the age of Absolutism. Incorporated into the *Académie Française*, and thus into a comprehensive theoretical discourse, architecture as a profession was gradually ennobled—a process which was not without consequences for the image of the architects, who came to be depicted in the form of an omnipotent aristocracy (183). It is no wonder that such a high evaluation of the architectural profession in turn incited imitation by royalty and princes. The ruler as an amateur, but influential "architect" of forms and arrangements became a trope of the Baroque (184, 185), and reappears in the guise of an "architect" like Adolf Hitler (see page xx) in the despotic abysses of the 20th century.

The architect as a suffering, lonely genius, rejected by society, is a vision of 19th-century Romanticism, seen in a figure like Karl

[185] The ruler as architect: Peter I (the Great) of Russia at the founding of St. Petersburg, painting by Alexander von Kotzebue, 1862.

Friedrich Schinkel, who to a certain extent purposely fostered this image after he graduated from the architectural academy and initially lacked commissions (but nonetheless earned a sizable income as a designer of theater sets). The idea of the architect as an autonomous artist is rooted in the Romantic era. Moreover, the entire understanding of art that arose out of late Humanism and remains in effect today is a product of this romanticizing approach. The architect as artist and creator of a unique work—from this point of view, Sir Norman Foster's demands, which strike against a vital and dynamic treatment of "his" architectural creation, are also understandable. Even if in current architectural circles modern forms of organization (networks of firms and highly specialized division of work, for example) predominate, the Romantic view of an architectural design as a "work of art" still remains powerful.

magnificent *Art Nouveau* station was converted with much sensitivity into a shopping center with adjoining hotel. Similarly, the Leon H. Blum House in Galveston, Texas, one of the few buildings to survive the catastrophic flood of 1900, was transformed from a department store into a flourishing luxury hotel. Abandoned waterfront complexes have been successfully turned into shopping malls to revitalize several decaying inner city areas, such as the San Francisco or Baltimore dockyards.

Defeated by history? Postmodernism

Reviewing the recent architectural past from the threshold of the third millennium one recognizes that aside from a number of more or less accurate slogan-like concepts (see page 156), only postmodernism signifies a coherent style. Long before it emerged in its present striking architectural forms, postmodernism was universally present as a theoretical model in architectural circles, signifying conscious abandonment of a depleted modernism—indeed, its opposite.

"Less is more" postulated Mies van der Rohe, one of the protagonists of the modern; "Less is a bore," Robert Venturi argued provocatively in *Complexity and Contradiction in Architecture*

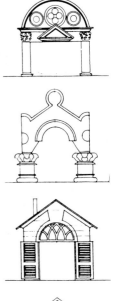

[186] Portal designs by Robert Venturi, 1977: An ensemble of historical alternatives as the basis for an "open" historical postmodernism.

(1966). Charles Jencks, along with Venturi one of the founders of the postmodern, invented this term for the new style of architecture in his many writings (*The Language of Post-Modern Architecture*, 1977; *What is Postmodernism*, 1984). The direction of the movement was clear: victory over and escape from the nihilistic, anti-traditional, misanthropic concept of the modern into an architectural style of "old" values—an architecture with ornamentation and color, symmetry, eclectic use of forms, historical references, harmony, and established formulas of value. Venturi's paradigmatic designs for a portal, reminiscent of the architectural model books of earlier centuries (186) in its composition, is an exemplary illustration of the background and consequences of this new historicism.

What has arisen from these precepts since the late 1970s is difficult to consider or describe neutrally. From the start, postmodernism drew mixed reviews. In this respect, it has had a revitalizing effect on present-day architecture by requiring every architect, critic, and architectural historian to take a clear stand on both its forms and its reactionary, backward-oriented ideological core. From the historian's standpoint, however, the result presents a dilemma for the understanding of the term today. Numerous supposedly architectural-historical publications stem precisely from the pens of the architects most involved in postmodernism (Jencks's books; Robert A. M. Stern's famous tract *Modern Classicism* from 1988). Moreover, important architectural historians have at times lost sight of their critical perspective in discussing the postmodern—a situation that makes a carefully considered understanding of this trend considerably more difficult for non-experts.

Venturi's portal designs indicated an almost historicist recourse to widely varying epochs of architectural history, which he treated as equally justified entities. In contrast, "applied" postmodernism soon narrowed its choice to a combination of the angular modern style and the ancient classical. Credited with igniting this modern classicism is the AT&T building in New York

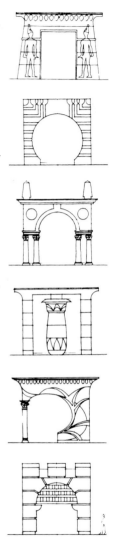

[187] The AT&T building in New York, a cornerstone of post-modern architecture. Architects: Philip C. Johnson & John Burgee, 1978–1983.

(187), constructed by Philip C. Johnson between 1978 and 1983. As a skyscraper, it belongs to the historical genre of the modern, but it looks back to the classical world in the symmetrical, pillar-like window arrangement of its facade and its "broken" gable as terminal roof element. The return to ancient classical forms of decoration, as well as their intentionally dysfunctional treatment, has become a trademark of the postmodern. In its full development, postmodernism becomes a playground of associations and irrationality, where extreme arbitrariness transforms discontinuity into an ideal and celebrates it. Typical are floating pediments; disproportional columns even standing on their heads; collections of classical motifs as if on display in a department store; a distortion of the classical canon of architecture even to the point of pseudo-significant inscriptions, of ancient appearance but laconically ironic content (*homo sapiens non urinat in vento* reads the classical Latin decoration on the portal of a postmodern apartment house in Amsterdam: "the wise man does not pee into the wind"). Here, history and historical forms have become histrionic, the plaything of an avant-garde that has distanced itself ever further from the real problems and threats of the world. "Anything goes" was not merely a slogan locked in architectonic stasis, but infected broad areas of the cultural scene. Postmodern poetry, philosophy, literature, film and even the humanities eagerly joined the fray, creating the mix of unrestrained eclecticism that was not only emblematic of popular culture, but also characterized serious essays and articles of the 1980s.

Criticism of postmodernism was immediate, massive, and firmly grounded. Particularly objectionable was the idea of a revision of the accomplishments of modernism. In the early 1980s, the renowned philosopher Jürgen Habermas discerned a threat to what he saw positively as modernism's attempt to create its own foundation—the attempt at an emancipation from the interweaving of historical conditions. In European intellectual circles, his penetrating arguments gained him the reputation of a spoiler arguing against an invincible trend. Today, however, even many former disciples of postmodernism have come to see the situation in a different light. Nonetheless, to reduce postmodernism to a harmless and short-lived stylistic joke would be a mistake. For the postmodernist attempt to revitalize the old, and to throw the accomplishments of modernism into question, has been all too deep. Its effect can be seen in the United States, where the present-day neoclassicism (see page 119, illus. 130) would be unthinkable without postmodernism.

In addition to the architects cited above, other significant practical and theoretical protagonists of postmodern architecture include Aldo Rossi, Michael Graves, Ricardo Bofill, James Stirling, Rob and Leon Krier, and Mario Botta.

[188] Classical architectural history, exhibited like goods in a department store, available to all: The Piazza d'Italia, an open plaza in the middle of New Orleans, designed by Charles Moore, 1977/1978.

173

Significant Architects

Significant Architects

Aalto, Hugo Henrik Alvar (1898–1976)
Most important exponent of the "nordic modern." Numerous buildings in his native Finland (incl. Helsinki House of Culture, 1955–1958), the United States (Residence Hall at M.I.T, Cambridge, Mass., 1947–1949), and in Germany (Cultural Center, Wolfsburg, 1958–1962; Essen, Opera House, 1959).

Adam, Robert (1728–1792)
This British architect and furniture designer, the most famous member of an architectural family, swayed English Palladianism in a neo-classical direction. Involved in the large-scale rebuilding of London along with John Nash, he also developed the Adelphi project near London together with his brother James (1730–1794).

Alberti, Leon Battista (1404–1472)
One of the great universal geniuses of the Renaissance, Alberti was also active as an architect in Mantua (San Sebastiano; San Andrea) and Rimini (*Tempio Malatestiano*), and as an architectural theoretician (*Ten Books on Architecture*, published posthumously). He stands as one of the founders of the classical emphasis in Renaissance architecture.

Apollodoros of Damascus
Roman architect and military engineer of the 2nd century AD, under the Emperor Trajan. He is credited with creation of the Trajan Forum in Rome.

Barry, Charles (1795–1860)
British architect, involved in the mid-19th-century neo-Gothic revival. He designed the Houses of Parliament (London, 1840–1860) along with his associate, Pugin.

Bernini, Gian Lorenzo (1598–1680)
Italian architect of the high Baroque whose works include the design of the colonaded piazza in front of St. Peter's in Rome.

Borromini, Francesco (1599–1667)
Italian architect of the high Baroque whose works (including *San Carlo alle quattro Fontane* and *Sant'Ivo della Sapienzia* in Rome) exemplify the complete victory of that style over Renaissance.

Boullée, Etienne-Louis (1728–1799)
An outstanding representative of French Classicism and the "revolutionary architecture" of the late 18th century. The conventionality of the few buildings he actually constructed (Hôtel Neuville Alexandre in Paris) stand in inexplicable contrast to his numerous futuristic and visionary, but unrealized, designs (including a cenotaph for John Newton in the form of a gigantic sphere).

Bramante, Donato (1444–1514)
Italian architect of the high Renaissance, Bramante was involved in the completion of the new building of St. Peter's in Rome.

Brunelleschi, Filippo (1377–1446)
Together with Alberti, the most important pioneer of Italian Renaissance architecture. His most outstanding work is the construction of the dome of the Florentine cathedral.

Chersiphron
Greek architect of the 6th century BC, heavily involved in the building of the Temple of Artemis in Ephesus, one of the seven wonders of the ancient world. He is credited with various inventions for the transport and placement of gigantic stone building elements.

Erdmannsdorff, Friedrich Wilhelm Freiherr von (1736–1800)
Pioneer of classicism in Germany, where he lent a Prussian accent to English Palladianism. His most important building project is the Palace of Wörlitz, near Dessau.

Fischer von Erlach, Johann Bernhard (1656–1723)
Imperial court architect in Vienna, and exponent of a "pathetic," absolutist, seignorial Baroque style. He authored *Entwurf einer historischen Architektur* (1721; "Proposal for a historical architecture").

Foster, Sir Norman (*1935)
English exponent of "Industrial Design." In addition to numerous buildings in the 1980s and 1990s in London, his consciously juxtaposed contrasts of historical building materials and industrial-like modern style are of particular significance. His works include the Library in Nîmes (1993) and the glass dome of the Berlin Reichstag (1997–1998).

Significant Architects

Fuller, Richard Buckminster (1895–1983)
American architect and engineer in high-tech direction. The stability of his geodesic dome is based on a triagular grid and represents the largest enclosable space with the least building material to date. His Dymaxion House design is a humanistic answer to Le Corbusier.

Gaudí, Antonio (1852–1926)
Eccentric Spanish architect whose works fall between Expressionism and Art Nouveau. His megalomaniac masterpiece, the Sagrada Familia cathedral in Barcelona (begun 1883), is still under construction according to his plans.

Gabriel, Jacques-Ange (1698–1782)
Most important French Baroque architect, pioneer of French "Baroque Classicism." Major works include the École Militaire in Paris (1751–1760) and the design of the Place de la Concorde (1755).

Gehry, Frank O. (*1929)
An important exponent of deconstructivism, his major works include the California Aerospace Museum (Santa Monica, 1985) and the Vitra Design Museum in Weil am Rhein, Switzerland (1987–1989).

Gilly, Friedrich (1772–1800)
An exponent of early German classicism, at age 23 he already taught at the Berlin Academy of Architecture, where he was the most important influence on Schinkel. Due to his early death, his work consists largely of designs and theory.

Gropius, Walter (1883–1969)
Founder of the Bauhaus; argued the functionality of the design as the "ultima ratio" to be sifted out from all earlier historical models, and applied this concept to architecture. Major works include the Bauhaus building (Dessau, 1925–1926) and the Harvard Graduate Center (Cambridge, Mass., 1950); he was also active in many other areas of design.

Haussman, (Baron) George Eugène (1809–1891)
An administrator commissioned by Napoleon III to modernize Paris by razing medieval "disorder" to create the now characteristic wide avenues and parks.

Hawksmoor, Nicholas (1661–1736)
Most important English architect of the Baroque and early historical Classicism. He designed numerous churches in London (including Christchurch, Spitalfields; mausoleum of Howard Castle) and was involved with Blenheim Palace.

Hippodamos of Milet
Greek architect and city planner of the 5th century BC. His concept of city planning based on orthogonal grids divided the city into rationally interlocking dwelling, economic, administrative, and religious areas, and was often copied by the postclassical world.

Hermogenes
Greek architect of the 3rd/2nd century BC. His Temple of Artemis of Magnesia on the Meander was a model of Ionic order.

Holl, Elias (1573–1646)
City building master in Augsburg; imported the architectural concepts of Palladio into the traditional southern German sphere, and designed the Renaissance masterpiece of the Augsburg City Hall with its 7-story gable flanked with towers (1615–1620).

Iktinos
Greek architect of the 5th century BC, credited with designing the Parthenon on the Athenian Acropolis, today the quintessential Greek peristyle temple (built 448–432 BC).

Isodoros of Milet
Late Roman architect of the 6th century AD. He built the Hagia Sophia in Constantinople (today Istanbul), famous for its huge domed central area.

Jefferson, Thomas (1743–1826)
Not only an agronomist and politician (United States president 1801–1809), but also an architect; his estate, Monticello, and the University of Virginia (both in Charlottesville, Virginia), which he built and financed, and the State Capitol (Richmond, Virginia) are the major works of an American classicism linked to Palladio and the French traditions.

Jencks, Charles (*1939)
American architect and theorist, author of The Language of Post-Modern Architecture (1984).

Johnson, Philip (*1906)
American postmodernist architect; his major works include the AT&T building in New York (1978). His exhibit "The International Style" in

Significant Architects

1932 did much to publicize postmodern ideas.

Jones, Inigo (1573–1652)
Together with Wren and Hawksmoor, the most important architect of England. Jones is the founder of English Palladianism and a central figure in 18th-century English neo-Palladianism (along with Lord Burlington and others). Major works: Queens House (Greenwich, 1616–1618) and the Banqueting Hall at Whitehall (London, 1619–1622).

Klenze, Leo von (1784–1864)
Court architect of Bavarian King Ludwig I; along with Schinkel, the fixed star of 19th-century German classicism. Numerous buildings in Munich (Propylaen, Glyptothek), the Valhalla (near Regensburg), and the Hall of Liberation (near Kehlheim/Danube).

Knobelsdorff, Georg Wenzelslaus (1699–1753)
Court architect to Frederick the Great; his City Castle in Potsdam (1744–1751) became a model for the Prussian Baroque.

Latrobe, Benjamin (1764–1820)
British architect, emigrated to the United States, where he became a leading exponent of the Greek Revival (see also Stuart). Latrobe built various classicist buildings in Philadelphia and is co-designer of the later building phases of the Capitol in Washington D.C.

Le Corbusier (1887–1965)
Pseudonym for Charles-Édouard Janneret. In addition to his "sculptural" buildings in the expressionist mode (Church of Ronchamp, 1950–1954), he became a controversial figure for his pioneer work in a "new objectivity." His idea of a "machine for living" that would serve all human needs (living space, leisure activities, work) inside a hermetically closed building (for example, Corbusier House in Berlin) was permanently discredited in the concrete brutalism of the 1970s; his basic principle aroused suspicion of fascism from various quarters.

Ledoux, Claude-Nicolas (1736–1806)
Extreme exponent of French "revolutionary" architecture around 1800. Ledoux created a "speaking" architecture influenced by a many-leveled recourse to ancient classical yet futuristic-seeming concepts for living and factory compounds, as well as state buildings intended to solicit observers' and users' submission by the use of various architectural and ornamental patterns. Major work: Salt works near Chaux. Numerous 19th-century prisons were inspired by Ledoux's formulations.

Lissitzky, Eliezer Markowitsch (1890–1941)
As a painter and designing architect, a central figure of Russian constructivism. His completely unrealized designs in the avant-garde style influenced Mies van der Rohe, among others.

Loos, Adolf (1870–1933)
Today seen as the most important Austrian architect of early modernism; his radical tracts against *Art Nouveau* ("Ornament and Crime," 1908) and his unique designs (Chicago Tribune Tower, 1922, in the form of a monumental Doric column) have aroused more attention than his rationally oriented buildings. His reputation remains controversial.

Mackintosh, Charles Rennie (1868–1928)
Scottish architect and artist, initially a protagonist of the *Art Nouveau* movement, but later turned to a rational but expressive style. Influenced continental architects including Olbrich and Josef Hoffmann. His important buildings include the Glasgow Art School.

Meier, Richard (*1934)
His "white" buildings (including the Museum of Commercial Art in Frankfurt-am-Main, 1979–1985; the High Museum of Art in Atlanta, Georgia, 1980–1983; the Des Moines Art center, 1982–1965; and the new J. Paul Getty Center in Malibu, California, 1984–1997) formed a recognized and important step away from the postmodern.

Michelangelo Buonarroti (1475–1564)
Renaissance architect and artist; decorated the Sistine Chapel and designed the dome of St. Peter's basilica after 1547.

Mies van der Rohe, Ludwig (1886–1969)
Perhaps the most influential architect of the 20th century, his idea of a cubist and rational building design reduced to a structural skeleton forms the basis of the

Significant Architects

high-rise concept as well as transparent pavilions. The fashionable flat-roofed architecture of the 1960s was also influenced by him, as was the form of the sky-scrapers built in the 1960s and 1970s in many large American cities. His major works include the campus of the Illinois Institute of Technology in Chicago (1938–1956)

Nash, John (1752–1835)
English architect and urban planner, major figure of late British classicism and histori-cism. He planned the extension of large parts of London under George IV, including Regent's Park and its surrounding terraces, and Regent's Street. He is famous for his gleaming white stucco-clad classicism, and infamous to the inhabitants of his buildings for their shaky construction.

Neumann, Balthasar (1687–1753)
His design of the prince-bishops residence in Würzburg is a flagship example of German Baroque palace design.

Niemeyer, Oskar (*1907)
Pioneer of modernity in Brazilian architecture. His design and con-struction of the capital, Brasilia (begun 1957), is a masterpiece of modern city planning.

Palladio, Andrea (1508–1580)
An important architect of the late Italian Renaissance; his numerous northern Italian villas quoted and varied the patterns of ancient models and had a decisive influence on later architecture. (see also Jones). He wrote

The Four Books of Architecture (1570).

Pei, Ieoh Ming (*1917)
Chinese-born American architect in the modernist/high tech tradition, commissioned with important buildings throughout the world. Significant works by Pei include the East Wing, National Gallery of Art, (Washington, D.C., 1978), the Bank of China Tower (Hong Kong, 1987), and the glass pyramid at the Musée du Louvre, Paris (Paris, 1989).

Pugin, Augustus Welby (1812–1852)
English architect active in the Gothic Revival. Together with Barry, he designed the Houses of Parliament (London, begun 1840), but died before the completion of the work.

Pytheos (4th century BC)
Ancient Greek architect influential in rebuilding the city of Priene (Asia Minor), along with public buildings there.

Rietveld, Gerrit Thomas (1888–1964)
The elegant simplicity of the houses and villas designed by the trained carpenter (Rietveld chair) in the 1920s–1940s served as prototypes of a rationalistic-modern understanding of archi-tecture. Rietveld's Schröder House in Utrecht (1924) ignited the *Bauhaus* movement.

Rogers, Richard (*1933)
British architect whose important buildings include the Lloyds Building (London, 1986) and the Pompidou Centre (Paris, 1977) with Renzo Piano.

Rossi, Aldo (*1931)
Italian architect of ration-alist and neo-classic

tendencies. His works include the Teatro del Mondo in Venice (1979) and the Gallaratese apartments in Milan (1970).

Saarinen, Eero (1910–1961)
Finnish-born American architect, son of Eliel Saarinen. Eero S. is known for his bold shapes, in particular sweeping curved lines. Major works include the TWA Terminal in New York and the Dulles Airport Terminal in Washington, D.C.

Saarinen, Eliel (1873–1950)
Finnish-born architect, founder of the Finnish romantic school, and the father of Eero Saarinen. After settling in Chicago, he turned to functionalism in skyscraper design.

Schinkel, Karl Friedrich (1781–1841)
Protagonist of Prussian historicism. As a student of Gilly, he first tended toward classicism (Berlin: Old Museum, 1822–1828), but also to the neo-Gothic (design of the memorial for Queen Louise, 1810; various churches). In addition to his actual works of archi-tecture, he produced many fictional designs (including a palace for King Otto I on the Athenian Acropolis, and visionary stage settings (Mozart's Magic Flute, 1815).

Semper, Gottfried (1803–79)
Important actor in Prussian classicism and historicism; from 1834 to 1848, professor of the Architecture Aca-demy in Dresden; then in exile. Semper's major works include the Opera

Significant Architects

House (1838/41 and 1871/1878) and the Oppenheimer Palace (1845–1848), both in Dresden. He wrote *Der Stil in den technischen und tektonischen Künsten*, ("Style in the Technical and Techtonic Arts," 2 volumes, 1860/1863).

Shaw, Richard Norman (1831–1912)
British architect influential in the return to classic-oriented Georgian styling after the Gothic and Tudor revivals. His work includes the Swan House (Chelsea, 1876).

Sinan (ca. 1497–1588)
Janissery, court architect of Turkish ruler Suleyman the Magnificent. According to surviving records, under command of the sultan he constructed more than 150 mosques, 45 mausoleums, 75 *madrasahs*, 31 caravansaries, 38 palaces, as well as other showpieces and private buildings in the lands under Islamic rule beginning in 1530.

Soufflot, Jacques-Germain (1709–1780)
Architect of the late French Baroque. Among other buildings, he built the Paris cathedral of St. Geneviève (1755–1792; later secularized into the Pantheon), which became an important model for American classicism around 1800. He was active in the rediscovery of the Doric Greek temple of Paestum in southern Italy. This proved to be a turning point in the acceptance of ancient classical models for contemporary building, which until then had

been based solely on Roman models, rather than Greek.

Speer, Albert (1905–81)
From 1934, the building inspector general, and later armaments minister, under Hitler. He designed numerous unrealized architectural showpieces for the Nazi dictatorship and formulated their architectural understanding. Carried out the New Reichskanzlei (Berlin, 1938/1939) and Zeppelin Field (Nuremberg, 1934–1937). He wrote *Remembering*, an autobiography with problematic exonerating passages.

Stirling, James (1926–1992)
British architect and member of the history faculty of Cambridge University (1964–1967). Originally an exponent of a thoughtful critical reworking of the modern in the post-war era, Stirling later became an influential protagonist of postmodernism. His works include the State Gallery in Stuttgart (1977–1982).

Stuart, James (1713–88)
English architect, who traveled with Nicholas Revett from 1751 to 1755 under auspices of the London Society of Dilettanti to Greece and sketched surviving ancient buildings, especially in Athens. His foible for the classic Greek architecture earned him the nickname "Athenian Stuart" and a reputation as a pioneer of the Greek Revival in England.

Sullivan, Louis Henry (1856–1924)
An American Chicago-based architect,

opposed to ornamentation. Sullivan is best known for his skyscrapers (including the Wainwright Building, St. Louis, 1899; Guaranty Building, Buffalo, 1894).

Tange, Kenzo (*1913)
His numerous spectacular designs and presentations combine Japanese traditionalist architectural forms with elements of the modern. Beginning in the 1980s, he also had numerous commissions in Europe (among them in Naples, Centro Direzionale).

Terragni, Guiseppe (1904–1941)
Protagonist of Italian *razionalismo*; leading member of the *Gruppo Sette*. His Casa del Fascio in Como (1932–1936) became an example of the "white modern" style, an architectural union of ancient and modern that was an important element in fascistic architecture under Mussolini.

Vanbrugh, John (1664–1726)
English late Baroque architect, co-designer of the grandiose Blenheim Palace for the Duke of Marlborough in Oxfordshire, and of Castle Howard in Yorkshire.

Vanvitelli, Luigi (1700–1773)
Baroque architect at the Bourbon court in Naples. In addition to numerous country villas (i.e., the Villa Campolieto near Ercolano) and city palaces in Naples, he designed the new royal palace near Caserta with its gardens and infrastructure (Palazzo Reale, 1751–1772).

Venturi, Robert (*1925)
American architect, pioneer of postmodernism.

Significant Architects

Influential through his writings, including *Complexity and Contradiction in Architecture* (1967) and *Learning from Las Vegas* (1972). His works include an extension to the National Gallery in London (1981).

Vitruvius (Marcus Vitruvius Pollio; 1st century BC)
Roman engineer, compiled first surviving survey of architectural styles. The rediscovery of his illustrated *Ten Books of Architecture* was seminal in the development of the Renaissance.

Webb, Philip (1831–1915)
English architect who spurred the development of private domestic architecture, including the Red House for William Morris.

Weinbrenner, Johann Jakob Friedrich (1766–1826)
Responsible for the renovation of the city of Karlsruhe into a classicist metropolis on the model of St. Petersburg. Further works: spas and drinking halls in Baden-Baden (c. 1810).

Wren, Sir Christopher (1632–1723)
Royal building master, trusted with direction of the rebuilding of London after the Great Fire of 1666. His masterpiece is St. Paul's Cathedral (1675–1710), based on the design of St. Peter's in Rome.

Wright, Frank Lloyd (1869–1959)
American modernist architect; a pupil of L. H. Sullivan. Wright's buildings were logically developed from the inside out, and aimed at fitting harmoniously into the landscape (for example, the Falling Water House in Pennsylvania, 1934–1937). His "ecological paradigms" made him into a fixed star of international architecture of the 1980s. His most famous late work is the spiral-shaped concrete Guggenheim Museum (New York, 1956–1959).

Glossary

Abacus
Quadratic or voluted headplate over a capital

Acropolis
"High city," from Greek *ákro* = high and *pólis* = city. Shrine located on a height or a naturally pro-tected settlement area in Greek cities

Acroterion
Ornamental or figured finial of a building, usually a temple

Adyton/aditum
see **cella**

Aedicule
Wall niche surrounded by columns for placement of a statue or painting

Alternating columns
Rhythmic alternation of columns and piers in the Romanesque basilica

Andron
Apartment set aside for men in a house; location of the symposium in a Greek house

Apse
Semicircular or rectangular extension of a room, often with a half-domed roof; equally common to Roman secular architecture (palaces, baths) and Christian churches

Arcade
Placement of arches on columns or pilaster supports

Architrave
Stone joist spanning a bay, resting on the abacus of the capital and in turn bearing further elements of the beams of a columned building (including the frieze and the cornice)

Archivolt
Molding around an arch found on Romanesque or Gothic recessed portals

Atrium
Roofless interior courtyard in ancient Roman houses; forecourt of early Christian churches bordered by columns

Attica
Balustrade-like wall along the rim of a roof; conceals the edge of the roof

Baptistery
Early Christian baptismal building with a baptismal font

Barrel vault
Vault with a semicircular cross section, built either of masonry or by means of wedge-shaped blocks

Base
Foot of an Ionic or Corinthian column or pilaster

Basilica
Market hall with several aisles in ancient Rome; in early Christian architec-ture, constitutes a basic church form, along with the central-plan building

Baths
Public baths of ancient times, including complex heating system

Bay
Spacing between the axes of two columns in a columned building, in contrast to intercolumnia-tion, which designates the open area between the columns at ground level. In Romanesque and Gothic architecture, also desig-nates a section of a vault

Bay window/oriel
Windowed extension of a room at the front of a building

Beehive dome
"False" dome constructed of overlapping stone slabs

Bossed ashlar
Stone block with a rough finish, also known as an embossed or rusticated ashlar

Bracket
Diagonally set wood member in a timber-frame

construction for the support of the framework

Broken pediment
Pediment or gable with a missing or broken center area; often found in Hellenistic-Roman and Baroque architecture

Cami
The large Friday mosque, as distinct from the *masjid*

Caminata
heatable room in a castle

Campanile
Tower standing separately in front of the main building of an Italian church

Capital
Head element of a column consisting of the echinus (cushion) and abacus (headplate)

Castle keep
see **donjon**

Castle of a monastic order
Seat of the Teutonic Order, combining monastery and castle

Catacomb
Underground, multi-story, privately administered burial complex, common since the 2nd century AD

Catholicon
Main church of an Orthodox monastery

Cavalier
High platform in a castle above the bunkers and the defensive passage at the top of the wall; used as an observation point or for the mounting of arms

Cella
Innermost sanctuary of a Greek temple, often subdivided into a main chamber, a vestibule (pronaos). and a rear room open either to the exterior (rear portico or opisthodomos) or to the interior (adyton)

Centering support
Supporting framework, or scaffold, used in the construction of arches and vaults

Glossary

Central-plan building
Building in which all elements of the ground plan are organized around a common center point, in contrast to the oblong shape of the basilica

Circus
see **hippodrome**

Citadel
Stronghold inside a fortified city

Clerestory
Upper area of the vessel (main aisle) of a basilica

Cloister
Passageways, usually laid out in a quadrangle around an inner courtyard; central area of a monastery

Console, corbel, bracket
Protruding, load-bearing stone support for arches, cornices, figures, etc.

Continued cornice
Beams or cornices that are continued around a wall projection, column, or pier

Corbelled dome
see **beehive dome**

Cornice
Crowning string course; final upper molding of the column orders that appears as the diagonal or gable course on the front of a building, or a horizontal course on the side

Crepis
Stepped sockel of a columned building

Crossing
The central area of a church formed by the intersection of the nave and transept

Cruciform church
Church laid out on the plan of a Greek cross with a dome above the intersection of the two axes

Decorative pointed arch
Decorative Gothic gable above portals and windows, often composed of tracery

Diazoma
Horizontal ambulatory corridor around the spectator area of a Greek theater

Dipteral temple
Peristyle temple with a double ring of columns

Divan
Official state chambers of an Islamic palace

Donjon
French term for the central tower of a medieval castle

Echinus
Protruding cushion of a capital on which the abacus rests

Entasis
Slight curve of a Doric column

Flèche
see **roof turret**

Fluting
Vertical hollow ridging on the shaft of a column, culminating in a pointed groin (Doric) or a shallow fillet (Ionic, Corinthian). Since the Renaissance, columns have often been made with only partial or no fluting

Frame construction
see **timbered construction**

Frieze
The alternating arrangement of metopes and triglyphs above the architrave on Doric temples

Groin vault
Vault formed by the intersection of two barrel vaults of the same height, and in which the cells, or upper sections, meet in massive groins opposite to the rib vault

Gymnasium
Building complex for sport training as well as literary and cultural education in ancient Greek cities; consisted of a *palaestra* (wrestling hall) with adjoining roofed colonnade, columned halls, and a track

Half-timber
see **timber-frame**

Hall church
Single-room church without side aisles

Harem
Private area of an Islamic palace

Heröon
Memorial building for a hero; in the ancient classical world, often the fictive grave of a mythical founder of the city

Hippodrome
Track for horse and chariot races; forerunner of Roman circus

Imperial palace
Royal residence of the emperor or his representative; the term "Pfalz" designates a palace in the medieval German realm

Impost
Protruding horizontal plate laid between the start of a vault or arch and the bearing column

Intercolumniation
see **bay**

Keep
Norman fòrt

Lantern
Roof construction admitting light, usually placed above a dome

Loggia
Open arched hall or passage in the Italian Renaissance

Megaron
Main room of Mycenaean palaces and early Greek houses and temples

Metope
see **frieze**

Mezzanine
Intermediate or partial story

Mihrab
Prayer niche in a mosque

Minaret
Tower on a mosque

Minbar
Pulpit in a mosque

Naiskos
Ancient classic small temple without a surrounding columned peristyle

Naos
Core area of a Greek temple, synonymous with the term cella

Glossary

Narthex
Vestibule of early Christian and Byzantine churches

Obelisk
Stone pillars drawing together in a point; ancient Egyptian form of memorial architecture

One-aisled church
see **hall church**

Opisthodomos
see **cella**

Orchestra
Circular area for dance and acting in ancient Greek theaters

Oriel
see **bay window**

Pagoda
Clearly distinguished variety of the stupa

Palaestra
Part of a gymnasium (see entry) consisting of a nearly square courtyard with its surrounding rooms. The palaestra served as a training area for wrestling and boxing

Pendentive
Suspended spandrel, usually of a spherical triangular construction, that allows the transition from a polygonal ground plan to the rounded form of a dome

Peripteral temple
Peristyle temple with a single ring of columns

Peristyle
Columned hall surrounding an interior courtyard around which the living and utility areas are grouped

Peristyle house
Stately and showy style of house originally found in Greece, and later often in Rome, in which the elements of the house are grouped around a colonnaded courtyard

Pfalz
see **imperial palace**

Piano nobile
Magnificently appointed story of a villa or palazzo, usually a high-ceilinged second floor

Pilaster
Shallow relief pillar with base and capital

Podium temple
Etruscan-Roman form of ancient temple, erected on a high podium and accessible by a broad exterior stairway

Pronaos
see **cella**

Propylon
Portal construction forming the impressive entry into a shrine

Protruding bay
Protruding portion of a building, usually placed at certain points of the facade for the sake of symmetry

Rib vault
At the groin (the intersection and crossover points) of a rib vault, the ribs carry the static pressure (weight) of the groin vault onto the four supports; the groin vault allows an extreme narrowing of the skeletal structure typical of Gothic cathedrals

Roof turret
Small tower positioned on the ride of the roof above the crossing and containing a bell in church buildings and monasteries; among the mendicant orders, it replaced the bell tower

Rustication
see **bossed ashlar**

Sail vault
see **rib vault**

Scene
Permanent on-stage building in ancient Greek theater

Site hut
Medieval association of workers for building projects, independent from the other guilds. Similar forms of organization were also form ancient classical building projects

Spoils
Pieces of a building that had been made for another building, and are being reused

Squinch
Arch with niche-like vaulting between two walls that intersect at a right angle; the arch conveys the angular lower structure into the rounded form of a dome; see **pendentive**

Star bulwark
Defensive complex built upon a large star-shaped ground plan

Stave church
Type of medieval Scandinavian church with a framework of masts and a stepped roof construction

Stoa
Long oblong columned hall with a closed rear wall

String course
Horizontal strip extending from the wall that distinguishes the horizontal structure (stories) of a building and organizes the wall surface

Stupa
Building for religious rituals in Buddhism, usually in the shape of a bell or tower

Stylobate
Surface on which the pillars of ancient columned buildings stood

Synagogue
Site of religious services in the Jewish community

Tambour
Cylindrical architectural element between the dome and an angular part of the building

Timber-frame construction
Wooden framework with clay or brick-filled compartmented walls; an upright beam construction with continuous vertical beams is distinguished from a frame construction with a bearing scaffold that rises story by story; the two

Glossary

constructions may also be combined

Tracery
Ornamentation based on the form of a circle, properly used to partition Gothic windows

Triglyph
see **frieze**

Workers' cottages
see **site hut**

Vault
see **beehive dome** (also known as corbelled dome), **groin vault**, **rib vault** (also known as sail vault), and **barrel vault**

Vertical construction
see **timbered construction**

Viaduct
Pier construction developed by the ancient Romans that allowed a road to span a valley

Villa
A luxurious domestic building in the countryside, especially in ancient Roman and Renaissance times

Volute
Snail-shaped spiral ornament on Ionic capitals

Bibliography

Selected Bibliography

Adam, Peter.
Art of the Third Reich.
New York: H.N. Abrams,
1992.

Andrews, Wayne.
*Architecture in New York:
A Photographic History.*
Syracuse, NY: Syracuse
University Press, 1995.

Andrews, Francis B.
*The Medieval Builder and
His Methods.* New York:
Dover, 1999.

Bach, Ira J. and Wolfson,
Susan.
*Chicago on Foot:
Walking Tours of
Chicago's Architecture.*
5th rev. ed. Chicago, IL:
Chicago Review, 1994.

Binding, Guenther.
*High Gothic: The Age
of the Great Cathedrals.*
New York: Taschen
America, 1999.

Blau, Eve and Troy, Nancy J.
(eds.). *Architecture and
Cubism.* Cambridge, MA:
MIT Press, 1997.

Blumenson, John C.
*Identifying American
Architecture: A Pictorial
Guide to Styles and
Terms, 1600–1945.*
Rev. ed. New York: W.W.
Norton, 1981.

Braham, A.
*The Architecture of the
French Enlightenment.*
Berkeley, CA: University
of CA Press, 1980.

Calloway, Stephen and
Cromley, Elizabeth (eds).
*The Elements of Style: A
Practical Encyclopedia of
Interior Architectural
Details from 1485 to the
Present.* Rev. ed. New
York: Simon & Schuster,
1997.

Cantacuzino, Sherban.
*Re-architecture: Old
Buildings/New Uses.*
New York: Abbeville
Press, 1989.

Crook, Mordaunt J.
The Greek Revival.
London: J. Murray, 1972.

Dinsmoor, W.B.
*The Architecture of
Ancient Greece.* New
York: Norton, 1975.

Fleming, John, et al. (eds.).
*The Penguin Dictionary
of Architecture.* 4th ed.
New York: Penguin,
1991.

Frampton, Kenneth et al.
*Japanese Building
Practice: From Ancient
Times to the Meiji
Period.* New York: John
Wiley & Sons, 1997.

Gössel, Peter and
Leuthäuser, Gabriele
(trans. by Judith Vachon).
*Architecture in the 20th
Century.* Cologne:
Benedict Taschen, 1991.

Harris, Cyril M.
*American Architecture:
An Illustrated Encyclo-
pedia.* New York: W.W.
Norton, 1998.

Hitchcock, H.R.
*Architecture: 19th and
20th Centuries.* New
York: Penguin Books,
1977.

Jencks, C.
*Modern Movements
in Architecture.* New
York: Viking Penguin,
1990.

Jestaz, Bertrand (trans. by
Caroline Beamish).
*Architecture of the
Renaissance: From
Brunelleschi to Palladio.*
New York: Henry N.
Abrams, Inc., 1996.

Johnson, Paul-Alan.
*The Theory of Architec-
ture: Concepts, Themes
and Practices.* New York:
John Wiley & Sons,
1994.

Kennedy, Roger G.
Greek Revival America.
New York: dist. by
Workman Pubs., 1989.

Kostof, Spiro.
A History of Architecture.
Oxford, UK: Oxford
University Press, 1985.

Kostof, Spiro.
*The City Assembled:
Elements of Urban Form
through History.* Boston:
Little, Brown, 1992.

Koulermos, Panos.
*20th Century European
Rationalism.* Lanham,
MD: Academy Ed. UK,
1995.

Kruft, Hanno-Walter.
*A History of Architectural
Theory: From Vitruvius to
the Present.* New York:
Princeton Architectural
Press, 1994.

Lawrence, A.W. and
Tomlinson, R.A.
Greek Architecture. New
Haven, CT: Yale Uni-
versity Press, 1996.

Lootsma, Bart, et al (eds.).
*The Art of the Accident:
The Merging of Art,
Architecture and Media
Technology.* New York:
Distributed Art Pubs.,
1999.

McKay, A.G.
*Houses, Villas and
Palaces in the Roman
World.* Ithaca, NY:
Cornell Univ. Press,
1975.

Murray, Peter.
*Architecture of the
Italian Renaissance.*
New York: Schocken
Books, 1986.

Murray, Peter and Stevens,
Maryanne (eds.).
*Living Bridges: The
Inhabited Bridge Past,
Present and Future.* New
York: Prestel, 1996.

Norman, Edward.
*The House of God:
Church Architecture,
Style and History.* New
York: Thames and
Hudson, 1990.

Pehnt, Wolfgang.
*Die Architektur des
Expressionismus.* 3rd
ed. Ostfildern-Ruit: G.
Hatje, 1998.

Pelt, R.J. *Architectural
Principle in the Age of
Historicism.* New Haven:
Yale Univ. Press, 1991.

Bibliography

Peterson, Andrew F.
Dictionary of Islamic Architecture. New York: Routledge, 1999.

Pierson, William H.
American Buildings and their Architects, Volumes 1 & 2. New York: Oxford University Press, 1970.

Rykwert, Joseph.
The Dancing Column: On Order in Architecture. Cambridge, MA: MIT Press, 1990.

Sanford, Trent E.
Architecture of the Southwest: Indian, Spanish, American. Tucson, AZ: University of Arizona Press, 1997.

Scarre, Christopher (ed.).
The Seventy Wonders of the Ancient World: The Great Monuments and How They Were Built. New York: Thames & Hudson, 1999.

Schulte, K. (ed.; trans. by Sean McLaughlin).
Temporary Buildings: The Trade Fair Stand as a Conceptual Challenge. TransStuttgart: Avedition, 1997.

Scobie, Alexander.
Hitler's State Architecture: The Impact of Classical Antiquity. University Park, PA: Pennsylvania State University Press, 1990.

Sparke, Penny.
A Century of Design. Hauppauge, NY: Barron's Educational Series, Inc., 1998.

Stierlin, H.
Encyclopedia of World Architecture. New York: Taschen America, 1996.

Toy, Maggie (ed.).
Beyond the Revolution: Architecture in Eastern Europe. Lanham, MD: Academy Ed. UK, 1996.

Tsonis, A. and Lefaivre, L.
Architecture in Europe since 1968. New York: Thames and Hudson, 1997.

Van Der Meer, Ron.
The Architecture Pack: A Unique, Three-Dimensional Tour of Architecture over the Centuries. New York: Alfred A. Knopf, 1997.

Ward-Perkins, J.B.
Roman Imperial Architecture. New York: Penguin Books, 1981.

Warnke, M.
Bau und Uberbau. Soziologie der mittel-alterlichen Architekture nach den Schriftquellen. Frankfurt a.M.: 1976.

Waterson, Roxana.
Architecture of South-East Asia Through Travellers' Eyes. Oxford, UK: Oxford University Press, 1998.

Wilson, Jones Mark.
Principles of Roman Architecture. New Haven: Yale University Press, 1999.

Wolfe, Tom.
From Bauhaus to Our House. New York: Farrar, 1981.

Zukowski, J. (ed.).
Chicago Architecture, 1872–1922: Birth of a Metropolis. Chicago: Art Institute of Chicago, 1987.

Index of Places and Buildings

Index of Places and Buildings

Index of Places and Buildings

Index of Places and Buildings

Index of Names

Index of Names

Index of Names \ Picture Credits

Picture Credits